The

Abingdon Worship
Annual 2016

CONTEMPORARY &
TRADITIONAL
RESOURCES FOR
WORSHIP LEADERS

The

Abingdon Worship
Annual 2016

Edited by
Mary J. Scifres
and B.J. Beu

Abingdon Press / Nashville

The Abingdon Worship Annual 2016

CONTEMPORARY AND TRADITIONAL RESOURCES
FOR WORSHIP LEADERS

Copyright © 2015 by Abingdon Press

This book is printed on acid-free paper.

ISBN 978-1-4267-9812-2

All lectionary verses and all Scripture quotations, unless noted otherwise are taken from the Common English Bible (CEB), copyright 2011. Used by permission. All rights reserved.

Scripture quotations marked Inclusive Bible are taken from *The Inclusive Bible: The First Egalitarian Translation* by Priests for Equality (Lanham, MD: Rowman and Littlefield, 2007). Copyright © 2007 by Priests for Equality.

Scripture quotations marked NRSV are taken from the New Revised Standard Version of the Bible, copyright 1989, Division of Christian Education of the National Council of the Churches of Christ in the United States of America. Used by permission. All rights reserved.

15 16 17 18 19 20 21 22 23 24—10 9 8 7 6 5 4 3 2 1

MANUFACTURED IN THE UNITED STATES OF AMERICA

Contents

April

May

June

July

August

December

Indexes

Online Contents

The following materials are found only in the Abingdon Worship Annual 2016 section at www.abingdonpress.com/downloads. Instructions on how to view these materials in your browser or download them to your computer are available at the site. PLEASE NOTE: This file is password protected (see page 309).

Introduction

Worshiping God is an awesome experience. Leading others in the worship of God is a holy calling and a humbling responsibility. As editors of *The Abingdon Worship Annual*, we speak with preachers and worship planners from a variety of worship settings who all share a common challenge—to live up to this holy calling as they seek to provide quality, integrated, creative worship for congregations yearning for meaningful connection with God.

The task of planning worship should be filled with joy and excitement, but it is often plagued by competing demands on our time and energies—demands that drown creativity and stifle innovation. To help worship leaders produce excellent worship in the midst of their busy schedules, we are honored to offer this resource.

Following the Revised Common Lectionary, *The Abingdon Worship Annual 2016* provides theme ideas for each liturgical day and the written and spoken elements of worship to allow congregations to participate fully in the liturgical life of worship. (Those who seek assistance with visuals and multi-media resources that many worship services require will find what they are looking for in an on-line resource at Mary Scifres Ministries: http://maryscifres.com/Worship_Subscription.html.)

For basic song and hymn suggestions, as well as on-line access to the hard copy materials, we include internet access for each worship service at abingdonpress.com/ downloads. See page 311 for instructions on accessing the download. The web link allows users to import printed prayers and responsive readings directly into bulletins for ease of use and printing. In addition to the hymn and song suggestions, the online link includes some bonus material: suggested hymns, worship website suggestions, and offerings for All Saints Day.

In *The Abingdon Worship Annual 2016*, you will find the words of many different authors, poets, pastors, laypersons, and theologians. Some authors have written for this resource before, while others provide a fresh voice. Since the contributing authors represent a wide variety of denominational and theological backgrounds, their words you will vary in style and content. Feel free to combine or adjust the words within these pages to fit the needs of your congregation and the style of your worship. (Notice the reprint permission for worship given on the copyright page of this book.)

Each entry provides suggestions that follow an order of service that may be adapted to address your specific worship practice and format. Feel free to re-order or pick and choose the various resources to fit the needs of your worship services and congregations. Each entry follows a thematic focus arising from one or more of the week's scriptures.

To fit the Basic Pattern of Christian Worship—reflecting a flow that leads from a time of gathering and praise, into a time of receiving and responding to the Word, and ending with a time of sending forth—each entry includes Contemporary Gathering Words, Call to Worship and Opening Prayer, Prayer of Confession and Words of Assurance, Response to the Word, Offertory Prayer, and Benedictions.

Communion Resources are offered in selected entries. Additional ideas are also provided throughout this resource.

Long time readers will notice that Contemporary Gathering Words are incorporated into the Invitation and Gathering section and often function as "Centering Words" that may be printed in a worship handout or projected on a screen. Use the words offered here in the way the best suits your congregation's spiritual needs, and please remember to give copyright and author credit!

Using the Worship Resources

Contemporary Gathering Words and **Calls to Worship** gather God's people together as they prepare to worship. Often called "Greetings" or "Gathering Words," these words may be read by one worship leader or be read responsively. Regardless of how they are printed in this resource, feel free to experiment in your services of worship. They may be read antiphonally (back and forth) between two readers or two groups within the congregation: women and men, choir and musicians, young people and old, etc.

Opening Prayers in this resource are varied in form, but typically invoke God's presence into worship. Whether formal, informal, general, or specific, these prayers serve to attune our hearts and minds to God. Although many may be adapted for use in other parts of the worship service, we have grouped them into the category "Opening Prayers."

Prayers of Confession and **Words of Assurance** lead the people of God to acknowledge our failing while assuring us of God's forgiveness and grace. Regardless of how they are printed, whether unison or responsively, Prayers of

Confession and Words of Assurance may be spoken by a single leader or led by a small group. Some prayers may even be used as Opening or Closing Prayers.

Litanies and **Responsive Readings** offer additional avenues of congregational participation in our services of worship. Think creatively as you decide how to use these **Responsive Readings** in your service of worship: in unison, by a worship leader alone, or in a call-and-response format. Feel free to change the title of these liturgies to sit your worship setting.

Benedictions, sometimes called "Blessings" or "Words of Dismissal" send the congregation forth to continue the work of worship. Some of these Benedictions work best in call and response format, others work best when delivered as a blessing by a single worship leader. As always, use the format best suited to your congregation.

We have provided a number of Communion liturgies as well, each written specifically to relate to the thematic and scriptural focus of the day. Some follow the pattern of the Great Thanksgiving; others are Invitations to Communion or Communion Prayers of Consecration for the celebration of the Eucharist.

We know you will find *The Abingdon Worship Annual 2016* an invaluable tool for planning worship; it is, however, one piece of the puzzle for worship preparation. For additional music suggestions, you will want to consult *Prepare! An Ecumenical Music and Worship Planner*, or *The United Methodist Music and Worship Planner*. These resources contain lengthy listings of lectionary-related hymns, praise songs, vocal solos, and choral anthems. For video, screen visual and secular song along with experiential worship ideas for each Sunday, subscribe to Mary Scifres Ministries' online resource, Worship Plans and Ideas (http://maryscifres.com/ Worship_Subscription.html).

As you begin your worship planning, read the scriptures for each day, then meditate on the **Theme Ideas** suggested in this resource. Review the many words for worship printed herein and listen for the words that speak to you. Trust God's guidance, and enjoy a wonderful year of worship and praise!

Mary J. Scifres and B. J. Beu, Editors
The Abingdon Worship Annual
beuscifres@gmail.com
Learn more about workshop and training opportunities through Mary Scifres Ministries at www.maryscifres.com

January 1, 2016

Watch Night/New Year
B. J. Beu

Color

White

Scripture Readings

Ecclesiastes 3:1-13; Psalm 8; Revelation 21:1-6a;
Matthew 25:31-46

Theme Ideas

Start with the end in mind. Where are we going, and how
do we get there? Matthew reminds us that our actions
have eternal consequences. If we truly want to change
our lives, we are charged to feed the hungry, clothe the
naked, visit the sick and imprisoned, and comfort those
who mourn. The new heaven and new earth may be in
our midst, but we need to treat each other lovingly if we
want to be part of it. In Ecclesiastes, God reminds us that
weeping, tearing down, and lying fallow will always be
part of the seasons and rhythms of life. As we look with
anticipation to the new year ahead, we place our trust
in the One whose glory is beheld in the new heaven and
new earth—the One who will wipe away every tear.

Invitation and Gathering

Contemporary Gathering Words (Ecclesiastes 3)

God walks with us through the seasons of life: Seasons of joy and hope, seasons of sadness and loss, seasons of hope and new life. As a new year dawns, God walks with us every step of the way.

Call to Worship (Ecclesiastes 3, Psalm 8)

O Lord, our God,
> **how majestic is your name!**

As we journey through life,
> **you are always with us.**

In seasons of rejoicing,
> **we do not laugh alone.**

In seasons of mourning,
> **we do not weep alone.**

When the heavens open up,
> **we behold your glory.**

O Lord, our God,
> **how majestic is your name!**

Opening Prayer (Matthew 25)

Eternal God,
> as a new year dawns,
> may our love for you be made known
>> in our love for one another.

Help us let go of past failings,
> even as we open our hearts
>> to the possibilities that lie before us.

Guide our footsteps,
> that we may live as your beloved children,
>> created but a little below than the angels.

Proclamation and Response

Prayer of Confession (Matthew 25)
> Holy God,
>> we have forgotten how to love.
> We praise you with our lips
>> but remain mute about the plight of others
>>> who suffer from hunger,
>>>> and lack of shelter and warmth.
> We lift up our eyes to delight in the starry heavens,
>> but turn our gaze from the homeless and the needy.
> Open our hearts to the welfare of others,
>> that we may live the promise
>>> of a new heaven and a new earth. Amen.

Words of Assurance (Psalm 8, see vv. 4-5)
> The psalmist questions:
>> "What is humanity that you are mindful of us?
>> Who are we that you care for us so deeply?"
> In loving delight, you answer:
>> "You are my children,
>> whom I have made but a little below the angels.
>> I have crowned you with glory and honor,
>>> and will always love you."

Response to the Word (Ecclesiastes 3)
> For everything there is a season. May this be a season of new possibilities, as we reflect on God's call to feed the hungry, clothe the naked, visit the sick and imprisoned, and comfort those who mourn.

Thanksgiving and Communion

Offering Prayer (Matthew 25)
Mighty God, as we bring you our offerings—
turn our upturned gaze toward your needy children,
that we may see the faces of those who hunger,
and those who are sick or imprisoned;
turn our deep aspirations for getting ahead
into a profound yearning to help the plight
of those whom society has left behind.
Only then may we truly see the face of Jesus.
May these offerings help heal our broken world,
and may they heal our very selves. Amen.

Sending Forth

Benediction (Ecclesiastes 3, Matthew 25)
Every season in life is a blessing from God.
We rejoice in God's blessings!
Every purpose under heaven can lead us into life.
We rejoice in God's purposes!
Every act of kindness to the least of God's children
is a kindness done to Christ.
**We rejoice in the chance to make a difference
in our world.**

January 3, 2016

Epiphany of the Lord

B. J. Beu

Color

White

Scripture Readings

Isaiah 60:1-6; Psalm 72:1-7, 10-14; Ephesians 3:1-12;
Matthew 2:1-12

Theme Ideas

Today's scripture readings are much more than a celebration of kings bringing tribute to the Messiah. They
are a promise of light to those who live in darkness;
a promise of righteousness to those who suffer at
the hands of others; a promise of grace to those who
are lost; and a promise of salvation to "outsiders" of
all shapes and sizes. Epiphany is a day to remember
that God's light and love shines for all, not just for the
"chosen."

Invitation and Gathering

Contemporary Gathering Words (Isaiah 60, Matthew 2)
A star shines in the night sky,
bewitching the eye with its splendor.
Why do our hearts beat with wonder?
A star shines in the black of night,
teasing the imagination with fanciful thoughts.
We are made from more than dust of the earth,
we are made from dust of the stars.
A star shines for all to see,
heralding the arrival of the star child.
A fire ignites within the soul,
illuminating the path of journeys to come.

Call to Worship (Isaiah 60, Psalm 72)
Arise, shine, for your light has come.
The glory of the Lord bathes us
in the brightness of the dawn.
Lift up your eyes and look around.
Our hearts rejoice in the glory of God's Son,
who defends the poor, and delivers the needy.
Christ is like rain that falls on mown grass,
like showers that water the earth.
Let us bring him sweet smelling gifts
and pearls from the sea.
Let us offer him hearts full of praise.
Arise, shine, for your light has come.
The glory of the Lord shines upon us.

Opening Prayer (Isaiah 60, Psalm 72, Ephesians 3, Matthew 2)
God of starlight,
disperse the darkness of our lives,

6

that we may behold the light of your love—
a light that shines in every corner of our
world.
Guide our footsteps in the paths of righteousness,
that justice may flourish and peace may abound.
Help us follow the kings of old,
that through our own journeys of faith,
we may behold the mystery made known
through the coming of your glory
in the infant Jesus. Amen.

Proclamation and Response

Prayer of Confession (Matthew 2)
Eternal God,
we celebrate the courage of kings
who left their homelands and their own people
to follow a star;
we marvel at their quest to honor a child
whose power was announced
in the heavens above.
We would do anything to be part of their story—
as long as it requires little effort
or sacrifice on our part.
Forgive our feet of clay, O God.
Open our shut-up hearts
to the mystery made known in Christ,
that others may behold in us
the blessings to be found
in journeys worth taking. Amen.

Assurance of Pardon (Ephesians 3)
The power of the living God
transforms our hearts of stone

into hearts of gladness and song.
The power of the living Christ
brings light and salvation
to those who turn to God.

Passing the Peace of Christ
As children of the light, and recipients of grace upon grace, let us share signs of peace with one another.

Response to the Word (Psalm 72, Ephesians 3)
The word of God is stronger
than the foundation of the earth.
Let those who oppress the poor tremble.
The word of God brings justice and righteousness.
Let the sinner repent and return to the Lord.
The word of God shines the light of salvation
into the dark places of our lives.
Let all those who love God shout for joy.

Thanksgiving and Communion

Offering Prayer (Isaiah 60, Psalm 72, Matthew 2)
Merciful God,
those who come to the light of your dawn
taste the healing waters of justice
that run down like an ever-flowing stream.
In offering these gifts,
may we commit ourselves
to acts of kindness and mercy,
in all that we say, and in all that we do.

Sending Forth

Benediction (Isaiah 60, Psalm 72)

Follow the kings of old and search for God's Son.

We go forth, following the light of the world.

Follow the magi in search of the child of peace.

We go forth, proclaiming hope and blessing to the poor and needy.

Follow the star to behold the glory of God.

We go with the promise of new life in Christ.

January 10, 2016

Baptism of the Lord
Joanne Carlson Brown

Color
White

Scripture Readings
Isaiah 43:1-7; Psalm 29; Acts 8:14-17; Luke 3:15-17, 21-22

Theme Ideas
Water. Fire. Spirit. They are all in these readings. Through these means, God names and claims us as beloved ones. It is important to stress this identity, this belonging to God in a deep and intimate way. God loves us with a fierce tenderness, no matter what. God claims us as God's own. That identity—sealed in water through baptism, sealed in fire through testing, sealed by the Spirit through growth and rebirth—this identity is transforming and calling us forth. Our only authentic response is one of love—love of God and of God's people. If we do this, we will never be the same, and the world will never be the same.

Invitation and Gathering

Contemporary Gathering Words (Isaiah 43, Psalm 29, Acts 8, Luke 3)

First water, then fire… all the challenges of life.

How do we get through?

The One who calls us by name gets us through.

We belong to God, and God loves us deeply.

That would really make a difference in our lives if we could believe it.

Well, then, open yourselves up.

Listen for the voice of God calling to your soul.

Listen to the whisper of Spirit touching your heart.

We will listen to all that God wants to say to us.

We want to believe.

Call to Worship (Isaiah 43, Acts 8, Luke 3)

The One who created us, formed and made us,

calls to us.

We are here to listen and respond.

God has claimed us and named us beloved.

We rejoice in this transforming identity.

Touch by the Spirit, washed in the renewing water,

and set aflame with God's love,

let us worship and praise our beloved God.

Opening Prayer (Isaiah 43, Acts 8, Luke 3)

Loving and caring God,

you call to us out of the waters, out of the fire,

and through the breath of the Spirit.

You call us to embrace our identity as your beloved,

to let this identity shape our worship,

and indeed, our very lives.

In trust, we open ourselves during this time of worship,
   that we might receive your transforming Spirit,
      and be touched by your never-ending love.
As we are brought into intimate experience of you,
   help us embrace our identity in you—
      that the world will know we are yours. Amen

Proclamation and Response

Prayer of Confession (Isaiah 43, Psalm 29, Luke 3)
Gracious and loving God, we are often fearful—
   fearful of what will happen to us;
   fearful for the state of the world;
   fearful of making you angry with us.
Help us in our weakness—
   to live unafraid;
   to live the way of Jesus,
      even when it is unpopular;
   to speak up for those silenced by society;
   to demand justice for those oppressed
      by hatred and prejudice;
   to open ourselves fully to your call,
      and to your love for us;
   to be vulnerable in love.
Help us to know, deep in our souls,
   that even when we pass through treacherous waters
      and consuming fire
         you will be with us to sustain
            and to strengthen us.
Help us know that by living your ways,
   we are named and claimed as your beloved ones.
Help us bring this message of radical, transforming love

and liberation to a world in need.
In your glorious name we pray. Amen.

Words of Assurance (Isaiah 43, Luke 3)

The voice of God rings out through the ages,
    telling us not to fear.
Beloved, we have been redeemed
    by this great and loving God.
We have been called by name and are God's forever.
Hear the voice of God singing through your soul:
    "You are precious and honored in my sight,
    and I love you."
There is no greater promise or assurance than this.

Passing the Peace of Christ (Isaiah 43, Luke 3)

Let us greet one another with the affirmation: "You are a
beloved child of God, precious and honored."

Prayer of Preparation (Isaiah 43, Psalm 29)

Naming and claiming God,
    may we be open to your voice
        speaking peace and love to our souls;
    may we be touched by your Spirit,
        as these words transform us.

Response to the Word (Isaiah 43, Psalm 29, Luke 3, Acts 8)

For the word of God in water...
For the word of God in fire...
For the word of God in wind and Spirit...
For the word of God, which touches our very hearts and
souls...
    We give you thanks and praise.

Thanksgiving and Communion

Invitation to the Offering (Isaiah 43, Psalm 29)
Named and claimed by God, we are called to embody
God's love and presence in the world. Our offering will
enable this church to be the voice that speaks love, that
speaks challenge, and that speaks grace to a world that
so desperately needs to hear this radical, transforming
message.

Offering Prayer (Isaiah 43, Psalm 29, Luke 3)
All that we are, all that we will become,
  and all that we have is from you.
As we present these gifts of money,
  we do so responding to your voice—
    a voice that calls us beloved, and precious,
      and honored.
We give you our very lives, and our complete love,
  as we promise to be the people
    you created us to be. Amen.

Sending Forth

Benediction (Isaiah 43, Psalm 29, Luke 3)
Go forth as God's beloved ones
  to share God's message of love and transformation.
Go as those who embody God's blessing and peace.
Go, strengthened by this naming and claiming God,
  to bring God's beloved community, here and now.
Amen.

January 17, 2016

Second Sunday after the Epiphany
Mary Petrina Boyd

Color

Green

Scripture Readings

Isaiah 62:1-5; Psalm 36:5-10; 1 Corinthians 12:1-11;
John 2:1-11

Theme Ideas

Both Isaiah and John speak of the transforming joy of
weddings. God transforms Israel from being "aban-
doned and desolate" into "my delight is in her" and
"married"; and Jesus transforms water into wine. In this
second Sunday after the Epiphany, much is revealed:
God reveals Israel's glory; the psalmist reveals that in
God's light, we see light; 1 Corinthians reveals the va-
rieties of ways that God's light is manifest in our lives;
and Jesus reveals his glory, as he turns water into wine.
Beyond wedding imagery, these readings show us that
God's gifts are abundant, as is God's faithful love. Ad-
ditionally, images of light abound: Righteousness is depicted as a light and salvation as a torch. Finally, these

texts depict images of flowing water: Rivers of pure joy and springs of life.

Invitation and Gathering

Contemporary Gathering Words (Psalm 36, John 2)
A party has been planned. The people are gathered and the table is set. Love flows abundantly. God's light shines upon us. Come, guests of honor, delight in God's goodness as we worship together.

Call to Worship (Psalm 36)
God's love is higher than the sky.
God's faithfulness reaches beyond the clouds.
God's righteousness is stronger than the mountains.
God's justice is deeper than the seas.
In God's love we are safe.
In God we find life and light.

Opening Prayer (Isaiah 62, Psalm 36, 1 Corinthians 12)
Loving God, in your light, we see light.
Waters of pure joy wash over us.
We are amazed by the abundance of your gifts.
Your love transforms our despair into delight.
Your Spirit has blessed this community
    with an abundance of gifts—
        gifts of wisdom, knowledge, faith,
            healing, and love.
You are ever faithful, ever just, and ever righteous.
May we delight in you always. Amen.

Proclamation and Response

Prayer of Confession (1 Corinthians 12)
Loving God, it's easy to feel superior to others,
    that our gifts make us better somehow.
Center us in your love,
    that we may rejoice in the gifts of others.
Ground us in your peace,
    that we may use your precious gifts
        to build a community of healing and hope,
        where justice is found,
            and where all walk in your ways. Amen.

Words of Assurance (1 Corinthians 12)
The same Spirit offers an abundance of spiritual gifts.
Each is important; each supports the common good.
Celebrate the many gifts that this community shares.

Passing the Peace of Christ (John 2)
Christ revealed his glory as he transformed water into wine at the wedding at Cana. Christ's glory is revealed in the lives that are transformed by his love. Look at those around you, see Christ's glory, and share Christ's love with one another.

Response to the Word (Psalm 32, John 2)
Jesus turned water into wine, and it was the very best wine. In like manner, God's love transforms our lives, that we might become reflections of Christ's glory. So come to God's party! Taste the goodness of God's love. Drink from the river of pure joy. And shine with the light of God's love.

Thanksgiving and Communion

Invitation to the Offering (1 Corinthians 12)

The Spirit has given us so many gifts to use for the common good. May we offer these gifts to God and our neighbor with joyful hearts, delighting in the abundance of God's love.

Offering Prayer (I Corinthians 12)

God of abundance, you have poured out your gifts
upon this community,
giving us what we need
to work for your justice and peace.
In gratitude and joy for these gifts,
we offer you the gifts of our living.
We offer the gift of our money
for your transforming work in the world.
We offer the gift of our lives
for the healing of all people. Amen.

Invitation to Communion (John 2)

Jesus revealed his glory at a wedding feast, pouring out an abundance of goodness and love in the water he turned into wine. So too, Jesus is present with us at this feast, revealing his glory. Come taste the goodness of our Lord. Come and drink deeply, delighting in God's love.

Sending Forth

Benediction (1 Corinthians 12)

We have different spiritual gifts, but the same Spirit.
We have different ministries, but the same Lord.

We have different activities, but the same God.
Go forth to use your gifts with joy,
   knowing that the One who is Spirit, Lord, and God,
    blesses you each and every day.

January 24, 2016

Third Sunday after the Epiphany
Laura Jaquith Bartlett

Color

Green

Scripture Readings

Nehemiah 8:1-3, 5-6, 8-10; Psalm 19;
1 Corinthians 12:12-31a; Luke 4:14-21

Theme Ideas

What kind of biblical contradictions are we stuck with
this week? Both Nehemiah and Luke tell stories of
words causing profound transformations in people's
lives. Yet, Psalm 19 describes creation singing God's
glory—without a single word. So which is the better
witness: words or actions? "Preach the gospel always,
and if necessary, use words." Although this quotation
is widely attributed to St. Francis, there is no evidence
he ever said it, and plenty of evidence that he was an
articulate preacher who used lots of words. Francis is
also credited with praying: "Make me an instrument of
your peace." These beloved phrases remind us that both
words and actions must go hand-in-hand, so that every

aspect of our lives—both words and actions—may communicate the love of God.

Invitation and Gathering

Contemporary Gathering Words (Psalm 19)

(During the reading of Psalm 19, project dramatic images of nature on a screen: a colorful sunrise, towering mountains, beautiful flowers, waterfalls, and so on. Read slowly, with plenty of silent spaces to simply look at the images.)
The heavens declare God's glory.
The sky proclaims God's handiwork.
One day gushes the news to the next.
One night informs another what needs to be known.
There's no speech, no word, no sound to be heard;
    but their voices extend throughout the world.
Their words reach to the very ends of the earth.

Call to Worship (Nehemiah 8, Psalm 19, Luke 4)

This day is holy to the Lord your God.
    The universe tells of God's glory!
On this holy day, we will eat good food
and share it with others.
    The universe tells of God's glory!
On this holy day, we will preach the good news
of God's love.
    The universe tells of God's glory!

Opening Prayer (Nehemiah 8, Psalm 19, Luke 4)

God of creation, your heavens and earth shout out
    the amazing news of your power and glory.
God of justice, your laws of mercy and goodness reveal
    your vision of harmony for all people.

God of love, your Son Jesus Christ proclaims
  the amazing news of your liberation
    for all who are hungry, poor, or oppressed.
May we join with all of creation
  to become your message of love to the world.
Amen.

Proclamation and Response

Prayer of Confession (Nehemiah 8, Psalm 19, Luke 4)
  Dear God, sometimes we are too good at talking.
  We talk about our desire for justice,
    but our actions bring poverty and oppression
      to those we claim to serve.
  We talk about our deep love for you,
    but we come up short when it's time to show love
      for those who make us uncomfortable.
    We talk about our commitment to serve others,
    but our busy lives make it hard to find the time
      to act as your disciples.
  God, help us turn our words into actions,
    that our very lives may become the message of love
      you have called us to proclaim. Amen.

Words of Assurance and Introduction to the Word
(Nehemiah 8:9-10)
  In the time of Nehemiah, when the people heard God's
  instructions read aloud, they began to weep. Perhaps
  they suddenly understood how miserably they had
  failed to live up to God's expectations. We don't know;
  the text doesn't say. It does say that Nehemiah said to
  the people:

"This day is holy....Don't mourn or weep....
Don't be sad, because the joy from the LORD is your
strength!"
We need to hear these same words today, for our strength
comes from the Lord. In God, our joy and our forgiveness is assured!

Passing the Peace of Christ (Psalm 19)
If the heavens can declare the glory of God without
words, so can we. Today, let us pass the peace of Christ
without using words. Use a simple touch, a smile, a hug,
a fist bump....Let the heavens inspire you to be creative
as you wordlessly communicate Christ's peace with one
another.

Presentation of the Gospel Reading (Luke 4)
Rabbi: Today at our synagogue service, we're delighted
         to have Mary and Joseph's son back with us. Je-
         sus will be reading from the prophet Isaiah.
*("Jesus" comes forward from his seat near the front; the rabbi
hands him a scroll. Jesus unrolls the scroll and reads.)*
Jesus: The Spirit of the Lord is upon me,
         because the Lord has anointed me.
         He has sent me to preach good news to the poor,
         to proclaim release to the prisoners
         and recovery of sight to the blind,
         to liberate the oppressed,
         and to proclaim the year of the Lord's favor.
*(Jesus rolls up the scroll and hands it back to the rabbi, then
sits down in his spot near the front, followed by a moment of
silence. Then Jesus says loudly, from his seat):*
Jesus: Today this scripture has been fulfilled
         just as you heard it.
(The rabbi looks at Jesus in shock.)

Response to the Word (Nehemiah 8, Luke 4)
(Begin the accompaniment to "Make Me a Channel of Your Peace," [#2171 in The Faith We Sing], and continue it quietly underneath this litany):
God, when we talk about justice,
help us become your message of justice.
When we talk about love,
help us become your message of love.
When we talk about peace,
help us become your message of peace.
(The song leader or other musicians can lead the congregation directly into the singing of "Make Me a Channel of Your Peace.")

Thanksgiving and Communion

Offering Prayer (Nehemiah 8, Psalm 19, Luke 4)
O God, we know true joy:
when we follow your law,
when we share our abundance,
when we show your love to others.
May these gifts serve as a proclamation of your glory,
and may these offerings put our words into action
as disciples of Jesus Christ,
in whose name we pray. Amen.

Sending Forth

Benediction (Nehemiah 8, Luke 4)
Go forth into this holy day
to proclaim God's message of peace.

Go forth into this holy day
    to share God's message of justice.
Go forth into this holy day
    to be God's message of love.

January 31, 2016

Fourth Sunday after the Epiphany
Jamie Greening

Color

Green

Scripture Readings

Jeremiah 1:4-10; Psalm 71:1-6; 1 Corinthians 13:1-13; Luke 4:21-30

Theme Ideas

"And the greatest of these is love" (1 Corinthians 13:13b). What better theme could there be for Christian worship? In his epistle to the Corinthians, Paul describes the attitude of love that should drive all of our relationships. His words are often used only at weddings, but they were intended as a guide for all people at all times. In the Hebrew Bible, we see God's parental love. For Jeremiah, it is the parent/child relationship that gives purpose and instruction. The psalmist reveals God's protective love, and our child-like need for it. A different kind of love emerges from the Gospel text. This is the love that speaks truth to power, even in the face of great danger. Love changes everything.

Invitation and Gathering

Contemporary Gathering Words (Psalm 71)
> We are in need of shelter and protection. We are in need
> of God. We are in need of Spirit and Presence. We are in
> need of God. We are in need of love and hope. We are in
> need of God.

Call to Worship (Psalm 71)
> Where can we go and seek refuge?
> **We've taken refuge in you, Lord.**
> Who can rescue us from the grip of the wrongdoer?
> **We plead our case to you, Lord.**
> Is there any place we can run to escape
> the spiritual dangers that surround us?
> **The Lord is our rock and our refuge.**
> Let us lift up our praise as we celebrate the deliverance
> found only in the Lord.

Opening Prayer (1 Corinthians 13)
> God of hope and love,
>> let your love shine upon us this day.
> Let your patience and kindness flow through us,
>> inspiring us to new depths of love and hope.
> Transform our love,
>> that we might overcome envy and resentment,
>>> and rejoice in justice and righteousness.
> Envelop us in your love,
>> that believing, hoping, and enduring
>>> may become our way of life
>>>> on the path of love.
> In loving hope, we pray. Amen.
> (Mary J. Scifres)

Proclamation and Response

Prayer of Confession (1 Corinthians 13)
> Divine Lord, our words often betray us.
> Our speech does not convey the harmony and love
>   you call us to live in our lives.
> Today we ask you to bridle our tongues,
>   that we may speak words of faith and justice—
>   the love languages for our age.
> Even when we fail, we know your love doesn't.
> Lead us into the path of maturity,
>   that we may grow up as men and women
>   called to follow the most excellent way.
> —*Or*—

Prayer of Confession (Luke 4)
> Lord Jesus, you come into our lives,
>   and you tell us the truth about who we are.
> *(Pause)*
> Some truth is painful,
>   but without truth, there can be no genuine love.
> *(Pause)*
> We assume that our goals are your goals,
>   even when we love our own success and comfort
>   more than your kingdom.
> We are sometimes jealous when you bless other people,
>   instead of reserving your blessings for us.
> When we love ourselves more than we love you,
>   please forgive us, Gracious God,
>   and show us how to love you and others
>   the way that we should. Amen.

Words of Assurance (1 Corinthians 13)
> Love keeps no record of complaints, trespasses, or sins.
> Love does not condemn.

Instead, love generates honesty and authenticity,
 and opens its arms to forgiveness and acceptance.
As we confess our sins, we find peace,
 knowing God has healed us with mercy and truth.

Passing the Peace of Christ (Psalm 71)
As the Lord welcomes us lovingly into this place of safety and refuge, so too let us welcome one another with signs of blessings and peace.

Introduction to the Word or Prayer of Preparation (1 Corinthians 13)
Now faith, hope, and love remain—these three things. We are compelled by these virtues to search ourselves and examine the way we live. Our relationship with the divine Spirit and with one another depends upon it. And the greatest of these is love. As we hear God's word today, may eternal love swell within our hearts and change us into the people God created us to be.

Response to the Word (Jeremiah 1)
God's word has come to us,
 calling us as God's own.
The hand of the Lord has stretched out,
 inviting us to embrace the word.
Rejoice, for we are the people of God.

Thanksgiving and Communion

Invitation to the Offering (1 Corinthians 13)
The apostle Paul tells us that without love, our gifts, our sacrifices, our service, and our knowledge, are empty. Today, we are invited to evaluate our relation-

ships with the Lord and with one another. We are invited to understand the offering today not as a collection, but as a token of the depth and commitment we have to the Lord Jesus Christ, his church, and to the world he loves so much. We are invited to move beyond sentiment and symbolism, as we demonstrate our love for God through the ancient practice of sacrificial giving.

Offering Prayer (Psalm 71, 1 Corinthians 13)

God of love, who is love itself,
> you care for us in so many ways.
You show us your love in the sunrise and snowfall.
You cover us in your loving embrace,
> with the gift of the church
>> and the words of scripture.
You protect us and shelter us with your presence.
You whisper words of loving affirmation in our hearts.
You give us the gift of love itself, your very life,
> that we might experience divine love forever.
Our gifts can never match your own,
> yet we offer them as a token of our commitment
>> to show love in everything we do. Amen.

Sending Forth

Benediction (1 Corinthians 13)

We have gathered in faith.
We have worshiped with hope.
Now, we go forth to share God's love with the world.

Additional Resources

Poem: "What Is the Love of God?"
> The love of God is like...
>> a mother's calming words
>> a father's strong embrace
>> a friend's laughing countenance telling my soul
>>> I am not alone in this world,
>>>> there are others who travel with me.
> The love of God is not like...
>> a list of joyless burdens
>> a symbol of power
>> a religion that spews hate and anger
>>> toward otherness, and makes God
>>>> in its own image.
> The love of God is like...
>> a safe place
>> a gift
>> a helpful note on life, love, responsibility,
>>> and death.
> The love of God is not like...
>> a competition
>> a salary earned
>> a scolding from abusive parents
>>> who are not happy with how you turned out.
> The love of God is like...
>> a perfect day
>> a one of a kind love
>> a relationship so wonderful
>> that words fail to do it justice.

February 7, 2016

Transfiguration Sunday
Joanne Carlson Brown

Color

White

Scripture Readings

Exodus 34:29-35; Psalm 99; 2 Corinthians 3:12–4:2;
Luke 9:28-36 (37-43a)

Theme Ideas

Let's face it, the transfiguration is kind of out there for modern times: Jesus glowing in the dark; two dead guys hanging in the air with him. And how did the disciples know it was Moses and Elijah anyway? What does this whole episode have to say to twenty-first century folks? It is not only Jesus who is transfigured. We, too, need to be transfigured by his life and his teachings. The key comes at the end of the story: God adding "Listen to him" after claiming Jesus for a second time—the first time occurring at his baptism. We are not to be so dazzled, that we, like Peter, miss the message. We are not to hang out in our mountaintop experience and build commemorative booths. We are to listen to Jesus, who

calls us through his life—teaching us the radical, transformative, transfiguring, active love of God and God's
people.

Invitation and Gathering

Contemporary Gathering Words (Luke 9)
Wow. Look at the glow!
   Cool. Let's build a commemorative shrine
   so we can hang out here and worship,
   not bothered by the world.
This is my chosen. Listen to him!
   He's told us all along to love and to serve God
   and God's people everywhere.
What should we do then?
   Worship the One who calls us to listen—
   to listen to Jesus and be transfigured people.
Then let's get to it. Let's worship and praise God
with our songs, our prayers, our presence, our gifts,
and our witness to this transfiguring, radical love.

Call to Worship (Luke 9)
We have come at Jesus' bidding,
to witness and to understand.
   We have been called by the transfiguring God
   to lives of love and service.
   We see. We listen. We understand.
Let our worship reflect the glow we witness,
that God's light, shining within us,
might be a beacon to a world lost in darkness.
   Let our light shine so that all can see
   and be led to the God of love and grace.

Opening Prayer (Exodus 34, Luke 9)
God of transfiguration, glow in our hearts this day.
 Teach us what the coming of your chosen one
  really means for our lives and for our world.
 Help us overcome our fear of what people will think
  if we truly lived and professed our faith.
 Call us from our mountaintop experience
  into the world that so desperately needs us
   and our message of radical love, grace, and hope.
 Empower us to truly listen to your chosen,
  to live his words, and to imitate his life,
   that we, too, may be transfigured this day. Amen.

Proclamation and Response

Prayer of Confession (Exodus 34, Luke 9)
God of Moses, Elijah and Jesus,
 too often, we just don't understand,
  we just don't get it.
We are sleepwalkers who awaken to a new reality
 that we just can't wrap our minds around.
We want to remain safe and secure,
 reveling in our mountaintop experience.
Forgive our mistaken attempts to build booths,
 when we should be empowered by the experiences
  of your leaders, prophets, and chosen one
   to live out our call to do and be
    what you call us to do and be
     in this hurting, desperate world.
Help us really listen to your transfiguring message
 of radical, transformative love,
  and forgive us when we veil your glory.

May our mountaintop experiences strengthen us
for work in your beloved world.
Help us follow Jesus down from the mountain,
and set our feet on your way. Amen.

Words of Assurance (Psalm 99)

When Moses, Aaron, and Samuel cried out to God,
God answered and was a forgiving God to them.
Know, understand, and believe that God hears us too
when we cry out for understanding, wisdom,
discernment, and, yes, forgiveness.
Know that the transfiguring God
will cause us to glow with God's love
and wrap us in forgiving, loving arms—
strengthening us for our work ahead.

Passing the Peace of Christ (Exodus 34, Luke 9)

Turn to those around you. See their glow. Take off your
veil so that you may glow with them. Take them by the
hand, look into their eyes and tell them: In you I see the
reflection of God's love and grace.

Words of Preparation (Luke 9)

God says: This is my beloved, my chosen; listen to him!
May we truly hear, understand, and be empowered to
journey from the mountaintop back to the world, transfigured.

Response to the Word (Luke 9)

For the word of God that transfigures...
For the word of God that empowers...
For the word of God that now lives in our hearts...
For the gifts of resurrection power...
We give God thanks and praise.

Thanksgiving and Communion

Invitation to the Offering (Exodus 34, Luke 9)
We come to the time in our worship when we can offer
back to God a bit of what God has given to us. We do
this in thanksgiving for mountaintop experiences and
for the strength they give us to answer our call. In gladness, we offer our gifts and our very selves for the work
of this transfiguring God.

Offering Prayer (Luke 9)
Jesus called us to the mountaintop.
We saw his glow.
We experienced the presence of others.
In thanksgiving for this
and for many transfiguring times in our lives,
we offer our gifts, our resources,
and our very selves.
May they be used to transform this world
into the beloved community. Amen.

Sending Forth

Benediction (Exodus 34, Luke 9)
We have been to the mountaintop,
we have been in the presence
of those who have gone before,
and we have been changed.
Go now as transfigured people,
endowed with understanding,
strengthened by prayer,
and empowered to glow for God.
Go into a world that needs the warmth of that glow,
that the world might be transfigured
in love and justice. Amen.

February 10, 2016

Ash Wednesday

Mary J. Scifres

Color

Purple

Scripture Readings

Joel 2:1-2, 12-17; Psalm 51:1-17; 2 Corinthians 5:20b–6:10; Matthew 6:1-6, 16-21

Theme Ideas

A heart that is centered on God is the call that flows through today's scriptures. God calls through the prophet Joel: "Return to me with all your hearts / . . . tear your hearts, / and not your clothing" (vv. 12-13). The psalmist prays: "Create a clean heart for me, God" (v. 10). Following today's Epistle lesson, Paul writes to the Corinthians: "Our hearts are wide open" (v. 11), and Jesus reminds us: "Where your treasure is, there your heart will be also" (v. 21). As we enter the Lenten season, we are invited to change our hearts, refocus on Christ, and return again to the One who loves us first and best.

Invitation and Gathering

Contemporary Gathering Words (Joel 2, Matthew 6)
A heart centered on God is the best gift we can give to ourselves and to God. God calls us to return from the distractions that pull us away from our center, and to focus this day on opening our hearts wide, so that love may flow freely in our lives.

Call to Worship (Joel 2, Matthew 6)
Return to God with all your heart, mind, and soul.
We turn our hearts to you, O God.
Return to this season called Lent—
a season of fasting and prayer,
reflection and introspection.
We turn our thoughts to you, O God.
Return to yourself, and to the treasure
that is Christ living within you.
We turn our souls to you, O God.
Turning and returning,
with heart, mind, and soul wide open,
let us worship the God of love.

Opening Prayer (Psalm 51, Ash Wednesday)
Change our hearts, O God.
Renew us with your Spirit of love and grace.
Wash away the dust and ashes
that cloud our vision
and burden our lives.
Guide us back to you,
that we may refocus once more,
and rest anew in the treasure of your love.
In your holy name, we pray. Amen.

Proclamation and Response

Prayer of Confession (Joel 2, Psalm 51)
> Our hearts are heavy when we turn away from you.
> We weep for the sins that separate us from love
> > and from one another.
> We mourn for the lost innocence of lives gone astray.
> Lighten our hearts, O God.
> Cleanse our lives with your mercy,
> > that our hearts may be restored
> > > and our lives reclaimed
> > > > by your forgiveness and grace.
> In Christ's name, we pray.

Words of Assurance (Psalm 51, Matthew 6)
> This is the true treasure:
> > Hearts that belong to God;
> > Christ, who holds our hearts;
> > and God, who holds our lives
> > in the very heart of holiness.
> May your hearts be light, dear friends,
> > for in the name of Christ,
> > we are forgiven and made new!

Passing the Peace of Christ (Joel 2, Psalm 51)
> Share hearts full of love and compassion, as you greet
> your neighbor with signs of love and reconciliation.

Introduction to the Word (Joel 2)
> Let us turn our hearts to Christ, as we listen for the word
> of God.

Invitation to Imposition of Ashes (Joel 2, Psalm 51, Matthew 6)
> This is a season of holiness and reflection.
> **We come to center our hearts on God.**

Return to God with your whole heart,
trusting in God's mercy and compassion.
We come to center our hearts on God.
Receive the gift of blessing, as you receive the ashes
that remind us of our many needs—
the need to return to God,
the need to refocus our hearts and lives,
the need to receive forgiveness,
and the need to offer forgiveness.
**We come, trusting that God knows
our every need.**

Thanksgiving and Communion

Offering Prayer (Joel 2, 2 Corinthians 6, Matthew 6)
We bring our gifts, our hearts, and our very lives
to you, O God.
Bless these gifts, these hearts, these lives,
that we offer to you and to the world
in your holy name.
Send us forth as your holy people
to bless others with hearts wide open with love.

Sending Forth

Benediction (Psalm 51, 2 Corinthians 6)
With hearts renewed, with lives restored,
we go forth to love and renew God's world.

February 14, 2016

First Sunday in Lent
Deborah Sokolove

Color
Purple

Scripture Readings
Deuteronomy 26:1-11; Psalm 91:1-2, 9-16;
Romans 10:8b-13; Luke 4:1-13

Theme Ideas
In gratitude for God's good gifts to us, we offer a portion
of what we receive so that it may be used to further God's
work. In Christ, we are not separated or distinguished
by where we come from, or by access to food, power, and
possessions. Rather, all receive God's blessings when we
believe God's promises and do God's will. We follow the
example of Jesus in worshiping God alone.

Invitation and Gathering

Contemporary Gathering Words (Psalm 91)
The Holy One is our refuge and our strength. Let us
worship the One who calls us!

Call to Worship (Psalm 91, Romans 10, Luke 4)
We, who live in the shelter of the Most High...
let us come and trust in our God.
God's word is near us,
on our lips and in our hearts.
We, who trust in God's promises...
let us come and rejoice in the power of the Spirit.
The Holy One is our refuge and our strength.
We have come to worship the One who calls us!

Opening Prayer (Psalm 91, Romans 10, Luke 4)
God of signs and wonders, God of power and love,
God of breath and life,
you make no distinctions between us—
distinctions of ethnic origin or race,
gender or identity, riches or poverty.
All who believe in you will be saved.
In you, we learn to trust the changing seasons—
giving thanks as winter turns to spring,
as long, dark nights give way to brighter days.
In you, we find the courage to turn away
from all that is false,
rejoicing, instead, in the constancy of your love.
You, who are our rock and our redeemer,
save us from falling into temptation,
as we turn our hearts to you. Amen.

Proclamation and Response

Prayer of Confession (Luke 4 adapted from NRSV)
Jesus said, "One does not live by bread alone."
Yet we are unwilling to fast and pray,
mistaking dead rocks for the bread of life.

Jesus said, "Worship and serve only the Holy One, your God."

Yet we are unwilling to surrender to God's will, mistaking worldly power for the power of divine love.

Jesus said, "Do not put the Holy One to the test."

Yet we are unwilling to wait in silence, mistaking the sound of our own voice for the voice of God.

God of power and life,

open our hearts to your never-failing love.

Forgive us when we refuse to place our trust in you.

Words of Assurance (Romans 10)

The Holy One is generous,

pouring out blessings on all who call on God's name.

In the name of Christ, you are forgiven.

In the name of Christ, you are forgiven.

Thanks be to God.

Passing the Peace of Christ (Romans 10)

With the word of faith on our lips and in our hearts,

we all are one in Christ.

The peace of Christ be with you.

The peace of Christ be with you always.

Introduction to the Word or Prayer of Preparation (Romans 10)

God of breath and life,

your word speaks to us

in every moment of our lives.

Open our minds to receive your word,
that it might be always in our hearts
and on our lips. Amen.

Response to the Word (Romans 10)
God of signs and wonders,
we have heard your promise
to save those who believe in your healing love.
When we face the time of trial,
help us remember your word,
and call on your holy name.

Thanksgiving and Communion

Invitation to the Offering (Deuteronomy 26)
As the Israelites brought the first fruits of their harvest, in gratitude for entry into the land of promise, let
us bring our gifts and offerings, in gratitude for God's
abundant grace in our lives.

Offering Prayer (Deuteronomy 26)
God of breath and life,
you create us and sustain us;
you love us and bless us this day.
Accept these tokens of our gratitude—
the overflowing of our grateful hearts.

Great Thanksgiving
Christ be with you.
And also with you.
Lift up your hearts.
We lift them up to God.
Let us give our thanks to the Holy One.
It is right to give our thanks and praise.

It is a right, good, and a joyful thing,
>   always and everywhere to give our thanks to you,
>   who hears the cries of the oppressed and afflicted.
As our ancestors in faith were wanderers,
>   making their home wherever they were welcomed,
>   you call us to celebrate the bounty we receive,
>   and to share it with those who wander in need
>   of your grace.
We give you thanks for milk and honey,
>   for clean water and blue skies,
>   for the yeasty fragrance of fresh bread,
>   and for the power to resist the evils that tempt us.
And so, with your creatures on earth
>   and all the heavenly chorus, we praise your name
>   and join their unending hymn:
> **Holy, holy, holy Lord, God of power and might,**
> > **heaven and earth are full of your glory.**
> **Hosanna in the highest. Blessed is the one**
> **who comes in the name of the Lord.**
> **Hosanna in the highest.**

Holy are you, and holy is your child, Jesus Christ,
>   who resisted worldly temptations:
>   to turn stones into bread,
>   to reach for earthly power,
>   to put you to the test.
On the night in which he gave himself up,
>   Jesus took bread, gave thanks to you,
>   broke the bread, and gave it to the disciples, saying:
>   "Take, eat; this is my body which is given for you.
>   Do this in remembrance of me."

When the supper was over, Jesus took the cup,
    offered thanks and gave it to the disciples, saying:
    "Drink from this, all of you;
    this is my life in the new covenant,
    poured out for you and for many,
    for the forgiveness of sins.
    Do this, as often as you drink it,
    in remembrance of me."
And so, in remembrance of your mighty acts
    in Jesus Christ, we proclaim the mystery of faith.
    Christ has died.
    Christ is risen.
    Christ will come again.

Pour out your Holy Spirit on our gathering,
    and on these gifts of bread and wine.
Make them be for us the body and blood of Christ,
    that we may be the body of Christ
    to a world that is filled with temptations.
God of signs and wonders, God of power and love,
    God of breath and life,
        we praise your saving, gracious name.
    Amen.

Sending Forth

Benediction
    Celebrate the abundant grace of God's unfailing love,
        sharing it with all who are in need of grace.
    And may the God who hears the cries of the oppressed
        give us the strength and courage we need
        to face every temptation
        as did our Savior, Jesus, who is the Christ.
    Amen.

February 21, 2016

Second Sunday in Lent

Mary J. Scifres

Color

Purple

Scripture Readings

Genesis 15:1-12, 17-18; Psalm 27; Philippians 3:17–4:1; Luke 13:31-35

Theme Ideas

Hope in the face of despair, trust in the face of fear, and faith in the face of doubt flow through today's scriptures. Jesus remains confident, even as the Pharisees warn of Herod's murderous desires. Abram believes God's promises of a child with Sarai, even as they grow older. Paul calls the Philippians to stand firm, even as enemies emerge and Paul's suffering in prison continues. The psalmist trusts in God's protection, even when facing danger and fear. Hope overcomes despair, trust replaces fear, and faith overcomes doubt, even on the journey to the cross.

Invitation and Gathering

Contemporary Gathering Words (Psalm 27, Luke 13)

Beloved children, gather together. Christ protects us as
a mother hen protects her brood. God shines light into
the shadows of our lives, while the Spirit empowers us
with hope and faith.

Call to Worship (Psalm 27)

God is our light, our salvation, and our hope.
God's light beckons us like a moth to a flame.
Lift up your head and see the bright light of love.
We look up, seeking the face of God.
Stand firm and trust this promise:
God is with us now.

Opening Prayer (Psalm 27, Luke 13)

Protector God, gather us under the wings of your love.
Strengthen us by the power of your Holy Spirit.
Shine with the bright wisdom of Christ,
that we may hear your word
and walk in your ways.

Proclamation and Response

Prayer of Confession (Psalm 27)

Evildoers are not only in our world,
they are in our hearts and in our lives, O God.
Protect us from the evils that would mislead us.
Strengthen us against the fears that terrorize us
and cause us to stumble.
Shelter us from of the destruction
and the sorrow in our lives.

Restore our souls, and lift us up
   to walk on the journey with you.
In Jesus' name, we pray. Amen.

Words of Assurance (Psalm 27, Luke 13)
God's goodness calls to us.
Christ's love gathers us here
   as God's precious children—
   beloved and protected by grace.
In the grace of God, we are all forgiven.

Prayer of Preparation (Psalm 27)
Teach us your ways, O God.
Open our minds and our hearts
   to hear your word.
Open our lives and protect our journeys,
   that we may walk with you
      each and every day.

Response to the Word (Psalm 27, Lent)
The journey to the cross is long.
   The journey of life is long.
The journey with God is challenging.
   The journey of life is challenging.
The journey of faith is a gift.
   The journey of life is a gift.
   On this long and challenging journey,
      we are not alone.
   Christ walks beside us.
Christ is walking with us even now.
   Thanks be to God for this marvelous gift!
—*Or*—

Response to the Word (Genesis 15, Psalm 27)
>God's mercy leads us into terrifying darkness,
>>healing our weaknesses
>>>and shining the light of love
>>>into the shadows of our lives.
>God is the light of our salvation,
>>securing a heritage in Christ's name.
>God does not leave us in ignorance,
>>but teaches us the ways of life and death.
>Let us choose life.
>(B. J. Beu)

Thanksgiving and Communion

Invitation to the Offering (Genesis 15)
>When you look toward the heavens and count the stars, know that the blessings of your lives are just as numerous. As the ushers receive today's offering, look inward and think of the blessings you have received, the blessings you have to share.

Offering Prayer (Psalm 27)
>Your goodness is all around us, gracious God.
>Thank you for strengthening us,
>>that we may to share a bit of your goodness
>>>with the world around us.
>Bless these gifts.
>Bless our lives.
>Bless us,
>>that we may share your goodness with the world.

Sending Forth

Benediction (Psalm 27)
Hope in the Lord,
our courage and our strength.
Trust in our God,
our companion on this journey of life.

February 28, 2016

Third Sunday in Lent
Rebecca Gaudino

Color

Purple

Scripture Readings

Isaiah 55:1-9; Psalm 63:1-8; 1 Corinthians 10:1-13;
Luke 13:1-9

Theme Ideas

Today's scriptures call us to look honestly at our own lives.
Are the things that we "eat and drink"—the things that
we take into our lives—truly nourishing us? Isaiah tells
of those who buy "bread" that is not bread. In writing of
the ancient Israelites who worshiped idols, Paul describes
them as sitting down to eat and drink, but this meal is the
prelude to destruction, not life. In earthy language, Jesus
tells of a fig tree whose only hope is the enrichment of
its soil, its food and drink. All of these passages call us
to the true food of God's wisdom, love, and mercy. The
invitation to dine and live—"Listen and come to me; / listen, and you will live." (Isaiah 55:3)—awaits our response:
Coming, listening, repenting, and living anew.

Invitation and Gathering

Contemporary Gathering Words (Isaiah 55; Psalm 63)
*(Think of serving Communion on this Sunday, and prepare
the congregation for this life-giving meal from the very start.
Have a huge loaf of bread on the table or several loaves of the
same bread—big, puffy bread that looks delicious. Also place
a big pitcher of wine or juice on the table. Think about including a pitcher of milk as well. Then place a pitcher of water
beside the baptismal font.)*

    One: Everyone who is thirsty, come to the waters!
*(Someone pours the water into the font with gusto! Splashing
encouraged.)*

    Two: If you have no money for food and drink,
          come just the same.
(Speaker gestures to the table.)

    One: We have wine and milk.
(Someone holds up the pitchers.)

    Two: We have the best of food!
          Good bread that satisfies!
(Someone lifts up the loaf of bread.)

    One: Come and live!
    All: **We are hungry and thirsty.**
          We come to be truly satisfied!

Call to Worship (Psalm 63)
O God, you are our God.
    We seek you, thirsting for you,
        as we would for a stream
        in a scorching desert.
We come to behold your power and glory.
    We come to hear of your love—
        a love that means more than life itself.

We come as guests to your rich banquet.
You are our God.
We seek you and are satisfied!

Opening Prayer (Isaiah 55, Psalm 63)
O God of Plenty, you set a banquet before us
that is generous and life-giving.
You serve us the very best foods—
your love and loyalty,
your faithfulness and strength,
your work that satisfies,
your deep wisdom,
and your abundant mercy.
You call us to this feast:
"Everyone who thirsts! Everyone who hungers!
Everyone who seeks! Come! Come! Come!"
You promise that this feast will satisfy us
as nothing else can.
And so we call out to you, O God,
for you are near, and we come! Amen.

Proclamation and Response

Prayer of Confession (Isaiah 55, Luke 13)
O God of every blessing,
you invite us into a life
of deep meaning and purpose,
a life of loving goodness and faithfulness.
We hear your invitation,
but are often distracted by other invitations—
invitations to things that don't satisfy,
things that waste our energy
and our purpose.

O God, renew your call within us—
    your call to all who hunger and thirst
        for ultimate value in their lives;
    your call to all who yearn
        for your powerful presence in their lives.
    Be merciful to us, forgive our sins,
        and give us new resolve
            to answer your invitation. Amen.

Words of Assurance (Isaiah 55, Psalm 63)

The prophet Isaiah tells us that we need only return
to the Lord our God, for God is merciful,
and forgives our sins.
    Your love means more than life to us, O God;
    we praise you!

Passing the Peace of Christ (Isaiah 55)

If a banquet is anything, it is a joyful sharing of the
host's love and generosity. As guests to God's feast, let
us greet one another with the love and peace of God,
through Jesus Christ.

Introduction to the Word (Isaiah 55:3 NRSV)

God calls out, "Incline your ear, and come to me!
Listen, so that you may live!"
    We have come to listen,
    for we are your people, O God.

Response to the Word (Isaiah 55, 1 Corinthians 10)

We have listened to your words, O God.
You have fed us with spiritual food
that satisfies our deepest needs.
    Your love means more than life to us, O God;
    we praise you. We will seek you as long as we live.

Thanksgiving and Communion

Invitation to the Offering (Isaiah 55)

God's banquet of love and mercy is generous beyond
words. God invites anyone and everyone who thirsts
and hungers for more in their lives. All are welcome
to this banquet. From our gratitude for God's nourish-
ment, let us give to others so that they may hear God's
invitation to life, and join us at the table of blessing.

Offering Prayer (Isaiah 55, 1 Corinthians 10)

Generous God, we thank you for your many blessings—
for keeping your promise of faithful love
across the ages;
for inviting us again and again—
through the prophets, through Jesus Christ,
and through this church today—
to share in the fullness of your life,
your love, and your power.
Remind us daily to hunger and thirst for you,
and for you alone.
And let us see this hunger and thirst
in those we encounter every day,
that we may tell them the good news:
There is an answer to the deep longing
in the soul.
Use our gifts today to spread this good news
to all who long for a deeper meaning
and a fuller purpose in their lives. Amen.

Invitation to Communion (Isaiah 55, 1 Corinthians 10)

(Be sure to serve fresh bread that people are encouraged to enjoy in big hunks. Act out the generosity of this banquet with
bread that satisfies—eye, stomach, and soul!)

Deep in your souls: Is anyone thirsty today? Is anyone hungry today? Are you tired of trying to satisfy yourself with things that don't really nourish you? Are you tired of spending your life's energy on things that don't fulfill you? Then listen carefully. The banquet to which we are invited today serves the best of food. It is spiritual food and drink that fills the soul with the presence and power and love of God. This meal can be the beginning of a new journey of meaning in all of our lives.

Sending Forth

Benediction (Isaiah 55, Psalm 63, 1 Corinthians 10)
We have feasted at God's banquet table.
This food fills our longings.
It gives our lives ultimate purpose.
It renews our energy for living!
O God, you have helped us and fed us.
We go forth, singing joyful songs!

March 6, 2016

Fourth Sunday in Lent
John van de Laar

Color

Purple

Scripture Readings

Joshua 5:9-12; Psalm 32; 2 Corinthians 5:16-21;
Luke 15:1-3, 11b-32

Theme Ideas

The call to reconciliation is at the heart of the Christian
way, and this week's lectionary readings. In Joshua,
the sign of circumcision reassures the Hebrew people
of God's forgiveness and love. It was this forgiveness
and love that liberated the Hebrews from the stain of
slavery and unbelief, an unbelief that caused years of
wilderness wandering. The psalmist proclaims that a
refusal to confess our sins and wrongdoing leads us to
pain and turmoil, but confession opens us to God's forgiveness and restoration. In the letter to the Corinthians,
the apostle celebrates God's gift of new life and reconciliation in Christ, calling believers to a ministry of reconciliation. Finally, the parable of the lost son describes a

father's willingness to receive his rebellious child back, and raises the question of how two estranged brothers might find one another again. The gospel is more than personal salvation—it invites us to participate in the world's healing, as we learn to give and receive forgiveness, and it teaches us how to be reconciled with God and with one another.

Invitation and Gathering

Contemporary Gathering Words (2 Corinthians 5, Luke 15)
> In Christ we are a part of God's new creation!
> In Christ we are reconciled with God
> and with one another!
> In Christ we, who were lost, are found;
> we, who were dead, are alive!

Call to Worship (Joshua 5, Psalm 32, 2 Corinthians 5, Luke 15)
> What joy is ours, when we reveal the truth
> of our lives to you, O God,
> and discover that we are forgiven.
> **What joy is ours, when we discover**
> **that we have been washed clean,**
> **and liberated from all that imprisons us.**
> What freedom we enjoy
> when our disgrace is removed,
> and we are reconciled to you and to one another.
> **What happiness we know**
> **when you open your arms to welcome us,**
> **and clothe us with your love.**
> We gather as those who are reconciled with God,
> and with one another.

As we worship you this day, O God,
create us anew in the power of your Spirit,
and fill us with new life. Amen.

Opening Prayer (Joshua 5, Psalm 32, 2 Corinthians 5, Luke 15)
Reconciling God,
you have ever been our guide and guardian.
When we are enslaved by the forces of evil,
you liberate us from bondage,
and remove the stain of our disgrace.
When we pray to you in times of trouble
and seek refuge in your strong embrace,
you come to us with songs of rescue.
When we follow the desires of our worst selves
and wander far from you,
you welcome us home with open arms.
When we need your wholeness and goodness,
you remove our sin and reconcile us to yourself.
Feed us again with your presence and grace,
and reshape us into new creations in Christ. Amen.

Proclamation and Response

Prayer of Confession (Luke 15, Joshua 5, 2 Corinthians 5)
O God, our Loving Parent,
we have allowed our impatience
and sense of entitlement
to drive us away from you.
We have squandered your gifts and goodness,
and have allowed our excesses
to rob us of life.
We have not acted as your children should.

Receive us back into the arms of your mercy,
    for our shame and disgrace
        are more than we can bear.
Help us this day to be reconciled with you
    and with our sisters and brothers. Amen.
(Time of silence may follow)

Words of Assurance (Luke 15, Joshua 5, 2 Corinthians 5)
Hear God's words of grace:
Bring out the best robes
    and put them on my returning children!
Put rings on their fingers
    and sandals on their feet!
Prepare a feast and let's celebrate,
    for they were dead, but now are alive;
    they were lost, but now are found!
Thank you, God, for your forgiveness
    and your faithful love!
Thank you, God, for rolling away our disgrace
    and making us new creations! Amen.

Passing the Peace of Christ (2 Corinthians 5)
In Christ, we are reconciled with God and with one an-
other. Let us share God's peace and reconciliation.
The peace of Christ be with you!
And also with you!

Introduction to the Word (Psalm 32, 2 Corinthians 5)
God says: I will instruct you and teach you
    the direction you should go.
I will advise you and keep my eye on you.
    Give us open ears, attentive minds,
    and receptive hearts to receive your word
    and be made new in Christ. Amen.

Response to the Word (Luke 15, 2 Corinthians 5)
God has welcomed us home,
and taken away our guilt.
In Christ, we are reconciled with God
and with one another.
We will be ambassadors of Christ,
sharing God's message of reconciliation
and participating in God's new creation! Amen.

Thanksgiving and Communion

Invitation to the Offering (Luke 15:31, 2 Corinthians 5)
The father said, "My child, you are always with me,
and everything I have is yours."
God has come to us in Christ, made us new,
and reconciled us to God.
Now we offer all that we have,
and all that we are,
to be ministers of reconciliation. Amen.

Offering Prayer (Psalm 32, Luke 15, 2 Corinthians 5)
For forgiving us and covering over our sin;
for rolling away our disgrace and feeding us
with your faithful love;
for reconciling us to yourself
and making us a new creation,
we thank and praise you, O God!
For blessing us with your goodness and grace;
for teaching us and guiding us
with your Holy Spirit;
for making us participants
in your reconciling work,
we thank and praise you, O God!

May these gifts be expressions of our gratitude—
    signs of our commitment to participate
        in your ministry of reconciliation. **Amen.**

Great Thanksgiving (Joshua 5, Psalm 32, 2 Corinthians 5, Luke 15)
    You who are righteous, rejoice in the Lord
        and be glad!
    You, whose hearts are right, sing out in joy!
        The one whose wrongdoing is forgiven,
            whose sin is covered over, is truly happy!
        The one free of guilt,
            in whose spirit there is no dishonesty,
            that one is truly happy!
    We thank you and praise you, O God—
        for making us a new creation,
        for removing the old self that holds us back,
        and for giving us new life.
    We thank you for coming to us in Christ
        and for reconciling us to yourself.
    When our impatience and selfishness
        drove us far from you,
        and we squandered your goodness
        in extravagant and foolish living,
        you welcomed us home with open arms,
        and removed the stain of our disgrace.
        You, who knew no sin, became sin for us,
            that we might become the righteousness
            of the living God.
    Your faithful love embraces us,
        and surrounds us with songs of rescue.
        In you we rejoice and are glad.
        In you our hearts sing out in joy!
        Hallelujah! Amen.

Sending Forth

Benediction (Luke 15, 2 Corinthians 5)
Go as those who have been made new.
Go as those who are reconciled with God.
Go as those who have been entrusted
with the message of reconciliation!
**We go as ambassadors of Christ,
seekers of the lost, revivers of the dead,
and participants in God's new creation. Amen.**

March 13, 2016

Fifth Sunday in Lent
Mary J. Scifres

Color

Purple

Scripture Readings

Isaiah 43:16-21; Psalm 126; Philippians 3:4b-14;
John 12:1-8

Theme Ideas

Today's scriptures call us to look forward rather than
backward, and to envision God's future instead of fo-
cusing on our past. The new things that God can do in
Christ Jesus are perceived through the eyes of faith—
eyes that are guiding us into God's future. For Jesus,
this meant turning his eyes and his path toward Jerusalem, even if that journey would lead to the cross. For us,
this means turning our eyes toward Holy Week and
the way of the cross, even as we trust in the promise of
"new things" and new life that arise from God's Easter
miracle.

Invitation and Gathering

Contemporary Gathering Words (Isaiah 43, Philippians 3)
God is always doing a new thing—creating a new day, calling us to new life, showing us a new path. Even as we journey toward the cross with Jesus, God calls us to reach forward into the journey that lies ahead.

Call to Worship (Isaiah 43, John 12, Lent)
God makes a way in the desert.
We will journey forward with Christ.
God promises new life in the face of death.
We will journey forward with Christ.
God restores hope for those in despair.
We will journey forward with Christ.
Come, let us journey in worship together.

Opening Prayer (Isaiah 43, Psalm 126)
Lead us, Lord, in this time of worship.
Make our paths straight and your presence clear.
Guide us with renewed hope,
that we may perceive the signs of life
that spring forth from your creative love.
With joy-filled trust, we pray. Amen.

Proclamation and Response

Prayer of Confession (Psalm 126, John 12)
Gracious God,
anoint us with your mercy and compassion,
as you hear the sins and sorrows of our hearts.
(Silent confession may follow.)

Guide us to be people who face anger and selfishness
    with anointing and healing power.
Guide us to be people who face doubt and despair
    with hope and determination.
Guide us to receive the new life that you offer,
    as we accept your forgiveness, and trust your grace.

Words of Assurance (Psalm 126, Philippians 3)
Forget what lies behind.
Trust in the path of grace that lies before us,
    for in the mercy of Christ's love,
    we are forgiven and invited into new life.

Passing the Peace of Christ (Psalm 126)
Share signs of joy and hope, as we pass the peace of
Christ together.

Introduction to the Word (Isaiah 43)
Listen for God's word, not by pondering ancient history, but by expecting new discoveries to emerge. Listen for God's word with expectation and hope, for God is always speaking a fresh word, always promising a new beginning, and always bringing forth new life.

Prayer of Preparation or Response to the Word (Isaiah 43, John 12)
Anoint us with your holy word, O God.
Bless us this day,
    that we may recognize the gift of your presence
        in our midst.
Help us see the new things you are constantly doing—
    in each of us, in your world, and in your church.
Anoint us with eyes of hope and compassion.

Thanksgiving and Communion

Offering Prayer (Isaiah 43, Psalm 126)
> You have restored our fortunes and given us joy.
> Bless this portion of our good fortune,
>> which we return to you now.
> With these gifts, and with our very lives,
>> bring forth new hope, new beginnings,
>>> and new life for your people everywhere.
> In Christ's name, we pray. Amen.

Invitation to Healing (John 12)
> As Mary shared her costly perfume with Jesus, Christ offers to us the precious gift of healing and hope. Come as you are. Come as you feel led, to receive this gift of healing and hope, offered in this time of healing prayer and anointing. May our prayers, and our gifts of healing, flow like the fragrant perfume of Mary … throughout this room and into the highest heavens.

Sending Forth

Benediction (Psalm 126, Philippians 3)
> God leads us into a new day on a new path.
> **We look ahead and see a new way.**
> Christ travels this road with us.
> **We go on this journey with Christ.**
> God is doing great things for us.
> **We go forth, rejoicing with hope.**

March 20, 2016

Palm / Passion Sunday
Deborah Sokolove

Color

Purple

Palm Sunday Readings

Psalm 118:1-2, 19-29; Luke 19:28-40

Passion Sunday Readings

Isaiah 50:4-9a; Psalm 31:9-16; Philippians 2:5-11; Luke 22:14–23:56 or Luke 23:1-49

Theme Ideas

In the space of a few days, Jesus is welcomed into Jerusalem with cheers and hosannas, only to be betrayed to his death on a cross. We are called to follow him, to walk with him, to eat and drink with him, and to pray with him, as he humbles himself in obedience and surrender. As Jesus did, we may ask God to take away our troubles. But ultimately, our calling is to accept God's will, rather than insist on our own desires.

Invitation and Gathering

Contemporary Gathering Words (Luke 19)

Blessed is the one who comes in the name of God. Sing and shout hosanna. For if we remain silent, the stones themselves will shout out in witness!

Call to Worship (Psalm 118, Luke 19)

Open the gates of justice,
that we may enter and praise God within them!
Here, at the gate of the Holy One,
we bring our thanks and praise.
Blessed is the one who comes in the name of God.
Blessed are you, who come to worship the one
who calls us and leads us into life.
We bring our thanks and praise to God.
For if we were silent, the very stones we tread
would shout out!

Opening Prayer (Philippians 2, Luke 22–23)

Gracious, sustaining source of all our days,
you invite us to follow Jesus as he enters Jerusalem—
to wave our palm branches in joyous greeting,
and to shout out our blessings and thanks
as he rides triumphantly through the
streets.
You invite us to join him at supper—
as he breaks bread and calls it his body,
and as he pours wine and calls it his blood.
As we wait with the disciples for a new dawn,
give us the strength to walk with Jesus,
who humbled himself
and became obedient to the point of death,
even death on a cross. Amen.

Proclamation and Response

Prayer of Confession (Isaiah 50, Psalm 31, Philippians 2, Luke 22–23)
> Gracious Teacher of love and compassion,
>> you call us to humble ourselves,
>>> even as you emptied yourself
>>>> to be born in human likeness.
>
> **We are rebellious and full of pride,**
>> **wishing to be thought of**
>>> **as your greatest disciples.**
>
> You call us to watch and pray,
>> to sit with those who are in anguish and despair.
>
> **Yet, in the long night of watching,**
>> **we betray you, refusing to help those**
>>> **who are weary with suffering.**
>
> You call us to live lives of love and service,
>> to follow you even to the cross.
>
> Forgive us Compassionate Teacher,
>> when we betray you with a kiss.

Words of Assurance (Isaiah 50, Psalm 31)
> The Holy One is gracious,
>> helping us in times of sorrow and despair,
>> forgiving even our worst trespasses.
>
> If the Lord God helps us, who will declare us guilty?
> In the name of Christ, you are forgiven.
>
> **In the name of Christ, you are forgiven.**
> **Glory to God.**

Passing the Peace of Christ (Philippians 2)
> The peace of Christ, whose name is above every name,
> be with you.
>
> **The peace of Christ be with you always.**

Introduction to the Word or Prayer of Preparation (Isaiah 50, Luke 22–23)
> Gracious Teacher of compassion and truth,
> > may we listen as those who are taught.
> Open our hearts to your holy word,
> > that we may find our courage and not falter,
> > > as we follow you to the cross and beyond. Amen.

Response to the Word (Luke 22–23)
> Gracious Teacher of truth and steadfast love,
> > you offer yourself to us,
> > > in bread broken and cup poured out,
> > > > even as you offered yourself
> > > > > to those who would betray and deny you.
> **Help us to follow you,**
> > **even when all seems lost. Amen.**

Thanksgiving and Communion

Offering Prayer (Luke 22–23)
> Holy One, you gave your life so that we might live.
> > **Standing at the foot of the cross,**
> > > **we offer you our love and our lives.**

Great Thanksgiving
> Christ be with you.
> > **And also with you.**
> Lift up your hearts.
> We lift them up to God.
> Let us give our thanks to the Holy One.
> > **It is right to give our thanks and praise.**

> It is a right, good, and a joyful thing,
> > always and everywhere, to give our thanks to you,

who sustains the weary, gives heart to the hopeless.
and leads us the on the road we should follow.
And so, with your creatures on earth
and all the heavenly chorus, we praise your name
and join their unending hymn:
Holy, holy, holy Lord, God of power and might,
heaven and earth are full of your glory.
Hosanna in the highest. Blessed is the one
who comes in the name of the Lord.
Hosanna in the highest.
Holy are you, and holy is your child, Jesus Christ,
who allowed himself to be broken on the cross,
pouring out his life so that we might have life,
and share it with a broken world.
On the night in which he gave himself up,
Jesus took bread, gave thanks to you,
broke the bread, and gave it to the disciples, saying:
"Take, eat; this is my body which is given for you.
Do this in remembrance of me."
When the supper was over, Jesus took the cup,
offered thanks and gave it to the disciples, saying:
"Drink from this, all of you;
this is my life in the new covenant,
poured out for you and for many,
for the forgiveness of sins.
Do this, as often as you drink it,
in remembrance of me."
And so, in remembrance of your mighty acts
in Jesus Christ, we proclaim the mystery of faith.
Christ has died.
Christ is risen.
Christ will come again.

Pour out your Holy Spirit on our gathering,
　　and on these gifts of bread and wine.
Make them be for us the body and blood of Christ,
　　that we may be the body of Christ
　　in a world that is broken and in pain.
To the One who gives us life,
　　the One who breathes within us,
　　the One who poured out life on the cross,
　　we give our thanks and praise. **Amen.**

Sending Forth

Benediction
　　Trust God. Watch and wait.
　　Be patient for the coming dawn.
　　And may the One who holds us all in steadfast love,
　　　　give us strength to follow Christ wherever he leads,
　　　　even to the cross and beyond.
　　　　Amen.

March 24, 2016

Holy Thursday
B. J. Beu

Color

Purple

Scripture Readings

Exodus 12:1-4 (5-10) 11-14; Psalm 116:1-4, 12-19;
1 Corinthians 11:23-26; John 13:1-17, 31b-35

Theme Ideas

This service is a time of solemn reflection on Jesus' last
night with his disciples. As we remember Christ's gift
of love to us, we are invited to listen to scripture, share
in Holy Communion and a foot washing ceremony, and
sing the songs of our faith. Jesus becomes a servant to
his followers—the ones who betrayed him, denied him,
and ran away in the face of danger. Jesus is an example
of faithful living in an age of unfaithfulness. The foot
washing ceremony depicts the depth of Jesus' love for
us and offers us a glimpse of true servanthood. How can
we fail to live up to his example?

Invitation and Gathering

Contemporary Gathering Words (John 13)

Called to love, called to serve, called to be Christ for
one another...they will know we are Christians by our
love.

Call to Worship (Psalm 116, John 13)

Come into God's presence,
with gratitude for the past and hope for the future.
   They will know we are Christians by our love.
Lift up the cup of salvation
and call on the name of the Lord.
   They will know we are Christians by our love.
Show one another love,
as Christ has showed us love.
   They will know we are Christians by our love.
Come, let us worship God, and love one another well.

Opening Prayer (Psalm 116, 1 Corinthians 11, John 13)

Fountain of holy love,
      as Christ showed great love for his disciples
         by washing their feet,
            may we show great love for your people
               by taking the role of the servant;
      as Christ satisfied the thirst of his disciples
      by offering them the cup of salvation,
            may we satisfy the hunger of your people
               with acts of mercy and compassion.
May everyone know that we are your disciples
      by our great love for you and for one another. Amen.

Proclamation and Response

Prayer of Confession (Exodus 12, Psalm 116, John 13)
God of the ages,
　　the Passover seems far removed from our lives,
　　　　yet the horrors of death,
　　　　　　and our need for your saving grace,
　　　　　　　　are ever around us.
We need your love to protect us,
　　your hope to guide us,
　　　　and your Spirit to complete us.
We need to feel, in our very bones,
　　your call to servant ministry
　　　　and the sense of rebirth
　　　　　　that comes from sharing your love
　　　　　　　　with the world. Amen.

Words of Assurance (1 Corinthians 11, John 13)
Jesus washed the feet and shared table
　　with those who would deny and betray him.
How much more will he share table
　　and offer forgiveness to us?
Lift up the cup of salvation
　　and call on the name of the Lord,
　　　　for we are blessed and forgiven by Christ.

Passing the Peace (John 13)
Just as Christ has loved us, so we should love one another. We are known as his disciples by our love. Let us
show this love as we pass the peace of Christ.

Response to the Word (Psalm 116, John 13)
We will pay our vows to the Lord in the presence of
God's people. We will pay our vows by loving one an-

other with the same love that we have seen and experienced in Jesus, the Christ.

Thanksgiving and Communion

Invitation to Foot Washing (John 13)
Loving Servant,
    on that night long ago,
        you knew that your hour had come
        and what lay before you.
Though your disciples loved and followed you,
    one would betray you,
    one would deny you,
        but all would fail you.
Yet, without judgment or resentment
    you got on your knees
        and washed their feet as a servant.
Tonight, we have come to have our feet washed—
    for we too have loved and followed you,
        and we too have failed you.
We cannot comprehend the love that heals us,
    the joy that completes us,
        and the grace that sets us free.
But we know that we need the Spirit
    of your love, joy, and grace,
        as much as we need the air we breath. Amen.

Invitation to Communion (Psalm 34, Psalm 116, 1 Corinthians 11, John 13)
Our souls hunger for food that satisfies.
    Taste and see that the Lord is good.
Our souls are dry and parched from thirst.
    Lift up the cup of salvation
    and call on the name of the Lord.

Our souls long for the bread of heaven.
Taste and see that the Lord is good.
Our souls yearn to drink of God' blessing.
**Lift up the cup of salvation
and call on the name of the Lord.**

Invitation to the Offering (Psalm 116)
With the psalmist, let us return to the Lord the many blessings that we have received. Let us pay our vows to the Lord in the presence of God's people.

Offering Prayer (Psalm 116, John 13)
Source of love and compassion,
    you fill us with a deep spiritual longing
        to taste the cup of salvation
            and know the joys of servant ministry.
In fulfillment of our vows,
    we offer you our very selves,
        that we may fulfill your law of love,
            and be known as your disciples. Amen.

Sending Forth

Benediction (Psalm 116, John 13)
Blessed by God, we are called to love.
They will know we are Christians by our love.
Blessed by God, we are called to serve.
They will know we are Christians by our love.
Blessed by God, we are called to be Christ
for one another.
They will know we are Christians by our love.

March 25, 2016

Good Friday
Mary Petrina Boyd

Color

Black or None

Scripture Readings

Isaiah 52:13–53:12; Psalm 22; Hebrews 10:16-25;
John 18:1–19:42

Theme Ideas

On this night, we remember the story of Jesus' betrayal, suffering, and death. We are forced to face the depth
of human cruelty and to acknowledge the truth of our
mortality. John's Gospel tells much of the story through
dialog, including extensive questioning. This service
lifts up the dialogues of John's Passion narrative. The
people respond with the words of Jesus, Peter, the Jew-
ish authorities, or Pilate. It may be done as a Tenebrae
service, with a candle extinguished after each reading.
Consider adding a time of silence or music between
each dialogue.

Call to Worship

Were you there when they crucified my Lord?
**We were the hollow echo of hosannas
once spoken in love.**
Were you in the garden when the disciples fell asleep?
We were the betrayal in Judas' kiss.
Were you in the courtyard when the cock crowed?
We were the denial in Peter's mouth.
Were you among the scoffers when Jesus was flogged?
We were the whip in the soldier's hand.
Were you in Pilate's chamber when he washed his hands
of Jesus' fate?
**We were the hatred of the crowd,
the indifference in Pilate's heart.**
Were you there when the soldiers dressed Jesus as a
king?
We were the mockery in the crown of thorns.
Were you among the spectators at Golgatha?
**We were the nails that pierced Jesus' hands and
feet.**
Were you there when they crucified my Lord?
We were the silence when no bird sang.
(B. J. Beu)

In the Garden: Who Are You Looking For?

Jesus and his disciples went to the garden to pray. Judas
brought soldiers to the garden to betray his old friend. Sol-
diers came to the garden, looking for someone to arrest.
Jesus asked:
Who are you looking for?
Jesus the Nazarene.
I Am, who are you looking for?
Jesus the Nazarene.

I told you, I Am.
If you are looking for me,
then let these people go.
Peter slashed out with the sword.
Put your sword away!
Am I not to drink the cup God has given me?

Peter Denies Jesus: Are You His Disciple?
At the high priest's residence, bystanders question Peter:
Aren't you one of this man's disciples?
I am not.
Surely you are one of his disciples?
I am not.
Didn't I see you in the garden with him?
No, I wasn't there.
The rooster crows.
We know we have denied Jesus.

Litany (John 18)
There is no warmth in the fire.
Our blood runs cold as the night.
The one we love is in peril.
Our courage blows away like the wind.
Strangers recognize our fellowship with Jesus.
Our denial pierces the soul
like the cock's crow pierces the dawn.
There is no warmth in the fire.
Our tears flow cold as the night.
(B. J. Beu)

Before the High Priest: Is That How You Would Answer?
The high priest questions Jesus:
We want to know about your disciples and your teaching.

I've spoken openly to the world.
I've always taught in synagogues
and in the temple, where the faithful gather.
I've said nothing in private. Why ask me?
Ask those who heard what I told them.
They know what I said.
Is that how you would answer the high priest?
If speak wrongly, testify to the wrong.
But if I speak correctly, why do you strike me?

Pilate and the Religious Leaders: What Charge Do You Bring?
Pilate questions the religious leaders who have brought Jesus to him:
What charge do you bring against this man?
If he had done nothing wrong,
we wouldn't have handed him over to you.
Take him yourselves and judge him
according to your Law.
The law doesn't allow us to kill anyone.

Pilate and Jesus: Are You King of the Jews?
Pilate questions Jesus:
Are you the king of the Jews?
Do you say this on your own,
or have others spoken to you about me?
I'm not a Jew, am I? Your nation and its chief priests handed you over to me. What have you done?
My kingdom doesn't originate from this world.
If it did, my guards would fight
so that I wouldn't have been arrested.
My kingdom isn't from here.

So you are a king?
You say that I am a king.
I was born and came into the world
for this reason: to testify to the truth.
Whoever accepts the truth listens to my voice.
What is truth?

Pilate and the Religious Leaders: Do You Want Me to Release Him?
Pilate responds to the religious leaders:
I find no grounds for any charge against him.
You have a custom that I may release one prisoner
for you at Passover. Do you want me to release for you
the king of the Jews?
Not this man! Give us Barabbas!

Litany (Matthew 27)
Jesus stands condemned.
Stop this madness.
It is too late.
We repent of our sin.
You have been well paid.
We don't want your blood money.
It is yours all the same.
Stop this madness.
It is too late.
(B. J. Beu)

Pilate and Jesus: Where Are You From?
Pilate asks Jesus:
Where are you from?
Why won't you speak to me?
Don't you know that I have authority to release you
and also the authority to crucify you?

You would have no authority over me
if it had not been given to you from above.
That's why the one who handed me over to you
has the greater sin.

Pilate and the Religious Leaders: Do You Want Me to Cru-
cify Your King?
Pilate returns to the religious leaders:
I want to release Jesus.
If you release this man, you are no friend
of the emperor! Anyone who makes himself
out to be a king opposes the emperor!
Here's your king.
Take him away! Take him away! Crucify him!
What? Do you want me to crucify your king?
We have no king except the emperor!

Prayer of Confession (Matthew 27)
Holy Mystery,
it is easier to wash our hands of responsibility
than it is to stand up for what we believe;
it is easier to defer to the judgments of others
than it is to take a principled stand.
When we take the easy way out,
forgive us, O God.
Fill us with the courage of your Son,
that we may cast off our darkness
and embrace your glorious light.
(B. J. Beu)

Crucifixion
Soldiers crucified Jesus and two others with him.
Pilate posted a sign:
Jesus the Nazarene, the king of the Jews.

The religious leaders complained:
> **Don't write, "The king of the Jews" but,**
> **"This man said, 'I am the king of the Jews.'"**

Pilate replied:
> **What I have written, I have written.**

Soldiers divided his clothing.
His cloak was seamless and they said:
> **Let's not tear it.**
> **Let's cast lots to see who will get it.**

The First Word from the Cross
Jesus said to his mother:
> **Woman, here is your son.**

Jesus said to the disciple whom he loved:
> **Here is your mother.**

The Second Word from the Cross
Jesus said:
> **I thirst**

The Third Word from the Cross
Jesus said:
> **It is completed.**

(Depart in silence.)

March 27, 2016

Easter Sunday
Joanne Carlson Brown

Color

White

Scripture Readings

Acts 10:34-43; Psalm 118:1-2, 14-24; 1 Corinthians 15:19-26; John 20:1-18 (or Luke 24:1-12)

Theme Ideas

How can we make Easter a day of surprises, a day of meaning, for people who think they have heard it all before? Easter calls us to be amazed at the power of our loving God and at the incredible gift that God has given us—new life, new hope. The women at the tomb did not expect what they saw and heard. But these women remembered and told others—the first preachers commissioned to bring the good news that marks us as Christians. We need to help people remember and be empowered to be witnesses in the world—even if what we say is dismissed as an idle tale. Jesus is risen! He is risen indeed! This declaration has become formulaic and is often spoken without great thought or feeling. But it points to a radical, life-changing reality that has the power to transform us all from our complacent, sleep-walking, church-going death, into newness of life. Easter allows us to make a difference in this God-blessed world.

Invitation and Gathering

Contemporary Gathering Words (Luke 24)
As the sun creeps over the horizon, you and two companions have come to anoint the friend you have lost— one last, sad act of kindness to the most beautiful and giving person you knew. Suddenly nothing is as you expected. Jolted out of your grief, you remember his promises. And in joy you run to tell the tale to others who loved him... only to be dismissed as speaking foolishness. Yet in your heart, you know that the experience of resurrection has changed everything—it has changed you, and it *will* change the world.

Call to Worship (Luke 24)
Jesus is risen!
Jesus is risen indeed!
Now say that again with conviction.
JESUS IS RISEN!
What does that mean for us?
New life! New hope! New us!
Come, let us worship our God who is full of surprises.

Opening Prayer (Luke 24)
Incredible, surprising, renewing, life-giving God,
we come this morning
to be shaken from our complacency
and our death-enduring routine;

we come to be shocked by this story
   of resurrection.
Open our eyes, hearts, and minds,
   to the amazing experience of resurrection.
May the birth quakes rock our world.
May we listen eagerly and expectantly
   to the women who bring this life-transforming news,
      even though we have heard it many times before.
Come to us, God.
Come to us, resurrected one.
Come in song, in prayer,
   in words of scripture and sermon,
      in the presence of our sisters and brothers.
Come and resurrect us. Amen

Proclamation and Response

Prayer of Confession (Luke 24)
We've heard it so many times before.
Jesus is risen: Yada, yada, yada.
We're just relieved the gloom of Lent and Holy Week
   is finally behind us.
This whole resurrection thing
   is a nice and pleasant fiction, but…
      we live in the real world.
Or so we tell ourselves.
Forgive our complacency.
Forgive us when we treat this day
   as a chance to dress up
      and go out for brunch.
Forgive us when we fail to remember
   what Jesus promised.

Forgive us when we think this doesn't have an impact
on our lives and our community.
Amaze us again.
Startle us anew.
Surprise us once more.
Fill us with resurrection power.
May we feel the birth quakes of resurrection
in our very souls,
that we, like the women who went to the tomb,
may go to share our faith,
even in a skeptical world. Amen.

Words of Assurance (Psalm 118)
God's steadfast love endures forever!
God hears and answers our prayers.
God has become our salvation.
Behold, we shall not die, but we shall live!
There is nothing more we need.
We have a witness in our heart
that we are deeply loved,
and in that love, forgiven.
It is marvelous in our sight.

Passing the Peace of Christ (Luke 24)
Turn to those around you and say: "May you experience
resurrection rampage and birth quakes of love."

Introduction to the Word (Luke 24)
As we listen to the Easter story once more, will we hear
an idle tale or life-giving words? The choice is ours.

Response to the Word (Luke 24)
For remembering...
For being amazed by this story...

For being brought out of our complacency...
For the gifts of resurrection power...
**We give thanks to the God
of resurrection rampage.**

Thanksgiving and Communion

Invitation to the Offering (Luke 24)
What can we offer in response to this amazing gift? We can offer our belief; we can offer our action; we can offer our resources and ourselves, so that the world may know the power of birth quakes.

Offering Prayer (Luke 24)
God of new life and power,
we offer all that we have,
and all that we are,
in amazed gratitude for the gift
of resurrection rampage—
in our lives, and in our world.
May these offerings be used
to shake, rattle, and roll the world. Amen.

Sending Forth

Benediction (Psalm 118, Luke 24)
We have experienced birth quakes!
We have experienced resurrection rampage!
We have been amazed, surprised, and gratified
to receive these experiences.
Go now in the name of the resurrected one.
Tell your tales and transform the world,
as you have been transformed. Amen.

April 3, 2016

Second Sunday of Easter

B. J. Beu

Color

White

Scripture Readings

Acts 5:27-32; Psalm 150; Revelation 1:4-8; John 20:19-31

Theme Ideas

Today's readings continue the great themes of Easter: resurrection, new life, and hope in the midst of profound fear and doubt. Revelation makes it clear that our hope is founded on the one who was, and is, and is to come: the Alpha and Omega. John affords a look at the role doubt plays in the life of faith. When doubting Thomas finds himself face to face with the risen Christ, he says: "My Lord and my God." Apathy, not doubt, is the opposite of faith. Doubt is an opportunity to dive deeper into our faith, and find our faith strengthened through the struggle.

Invitation and Gathering

Contemporary Gathering Words (John 20)

The risen Lord is among us. Put aside uncertainty. Put aside doubt. Put aside skepticism. Put aside mistrust. Do not doubt, but believe.

Call to Worship (Psalm 150)

Praise God in the sanctuary.
Praise God in the mighty firmament.
Praise God with trumpet and horn.
Praise God with lute and harp.
Praise God with tambourine and dance.
Praise the Lord with strings and pipes.
Praise God with clashing cymbals.
Praise God with beating drums.
Let everything that breathes praise the Lord!
Praise the Lord.

Opening Prayer (Revelation 1)

Eternal God, who was and is and is to come,
　　you are Alpha and Omega,
　　　　our beginning and our end.
In you, O God, we move and have our being.
Be the foundation of our strength,
　　as we seek to bring your kingdom here on earth.
Be the foundation of our courage,
　　as proclaim your glory for all to hear.
We ask this in the name of the one
　　who conquered the grave
　　　　to bring us eternal life. Amen.

Proclamation and Response

Prayer of Confession (Psalm 150, John 20)

God of earth and sky,
    your enduring love is like a mighty glacier
        that pushes aside all that stands before it.
Be patient with us as we strive to embrace
    the promise of our faith.
Like Thomas before us,
    we long to believe in the power of your resurrection,
        but so many doubts remain.
Faced with the ravages of hate,
    love seems like a candle in the wind.
We cleave to the promise of life,
    but death keeps hold of us still.
Come to us, in the midst of our doubt,
    that we may see Christ's glory
        and proclaim with Thomas:
        "My Lord and my God!"
            and taste the fullness of life. Amen.

Words of Assurance (Revelation 1)

The power of God's love heals us.
The power of Christ's love saves us!
The power of the Spirit's love sets us free!

Passing the Peace (John 20)

Even when they were afraid, the disciples gathered together for mutual love and support. Let us show the same love and support for one another as we share Christ's greeting: "Peace be with you."

Response to the Word (Psalm 116, John 13)

Give us eyes to see, O God,
    that our doubt may be transformed into faith,

and our fear may give way to courage
> as we share your good news with the world.

Thanksgiving and Communion

Invitation to the Offering (Acts 5)
As witnesses to the transforming power of God in our lives, let us be generous in our giving, that others may draw life from the bounty of God's blessings.

Offering Prayer (Revelation 1, John 20)
Alpha and Omega, Beginning and End,
> you are the source of every blessing.
In gratitude for bringing peace to our lives,
> receive these offerings as signs of our commitment
> to live as your faithful disciples. Amen.

Sending Forth

Benediction (John 20)
See and believe.
> **We go with our eyes newly opened.**
See and believe.
> **We go with our doubt transformed by faith.**
See and believe.
> **We go with our sorrow replaced by joy.**
Go with God's blessing.

April 10, 2016

Third Sunday of Easter
Native American Awareness Sunday
Mary J. Scifres

Color

White

Scripture Readings

Acts 9:1-6 (7-20); Psalm 30; Revelation 5:11-14;
John 21:1-19

Theme Ideas

Each of today's scriptures easily stands alone. Taken together, they point to the new perspective we find when we encounter the risen Christ. After encountering Jesus on the road to Damascus, Saul sees his calling very differently. After they recognize the resurrected Jesus in a meal on a familiar shore, Peter and the disciples are given a clear mission to feed God's sheep. John sees all creatures of heaven and earth praising Christ, and even the psalmist finds joy in the morning after a night of sorrow. This season of resurrection brings many new perspectives as new life is discovered.

Invitation and Gathering

Contemporary Gathering Words (Acts 9, Revelation 5, John 21, Easter)

Walking on a familiar road, fishing on a well-known beach, or singing a beloved song, we may yet encounter a new perspective. Open your eyes. Christ is here. Look to the heavens. The angels are singing. Search within. God is there. See what this new day may bring!

Call to Worship (Psalm 30, John 21)

The day has dawned.
Sing a new song!
Christ is alive.
Rejoice in new life!
With open minds and Easter faith,
come to worship God!

Opening Prayer (Acts 9, John 21)

Feed us with your word, Jesus.
With new perspectives,
and a vision of your presence,
refresh our hearts this day.
Be present in our midst,
that we might hear your voice
and respond to your call. Amen.

Proclamation and Response

Prayer of Confession

When we deny you, and follow paths that destroy...
Forgive us, Christ Jesus.
When we hide our eyes, and neglect your truth...

Forgive us, Christ Jesus.
When we miss your presence in our very midst …
Forgive us, Christ Jesus.
Feed us with your grace, merciful one.
Nourish us with a new perspective,
that we might see you in our very lives,
and nourish your world with love.
In your gracious name, we pray. **Amen.**

Words of Assurance (Psalm 30, John 21)
Though we have borne the long night
of suffering and sorrow,
joy comes with the dawn of God's mercy.
The light of the Risen Christ shines with the dawn.
Rejoice in this Easter promise!
We are forgiven and given new life in Christ!

Passing the Peace of Christ (John 21)
Peace be with you.
And also with you!
The peace of the Risen Christ be with us all.

Response to the Word (John 21)
Jesus is here, sharing his life and love.
Most assuredly, we truly love him!
Then feed the sheep of God's pasture.
Most assuredly, we truly love him!
Then care for the sheep of God's flock.
Most assuredly, we truly love him!
Then tend the lambs of God.
Most assuredly, we will love our God,
feed God's sheep, and tend Christ's lambs!

Thanksgiving and Communion

Invitation to the Offering (John 21)
> Let us bring loaves and fish, gifts and offerings, and
> lives of love for the sheep of God's world.

Offering Prayer (John 21)
> With your love, holy Shepherd,
>> help us to love your world.
> With your nourishment,
>> help us feed your world.
> With your guidance,
>> help us care for your world,
>>> all of its peoples,
>>>> and all of its creatures.
> With these gifts,
>> bring new life where it is needed most.

Invitation to Communion (John 21)
> Come and eat! Christ has prepared a feast of love and
> grace for all.

Communion Prayer (John 21)
> Be present in these gifts, Risen Christ.
> Restore new life within us
>> through the sharing of this bread and wine,
>>> that we may taste the new life you offer.
> Become new life for us
>> through the sharing of our friendship and love,
>>> that we may bring new hope to your world.
> Breathe new life among us
>> through the movement of your Spirit,
>>> that we may touch unity and peace,
>>>> and the power of your love and grace.

Become new life in our lives,
    that we may feed your sheep
    and tend your lambs.
In your holy name, we pray. Amen.

Sending Forth

Benediction (Acts 9, John 21)
    Go forth to proclaim new life!
    Go forth to proclaim the Risen Christ!
    Go forth to feed the world with love!

April 17, 2016

Fourth Sunday of Easter
Rebecca E. Garrett

Color

White

Scripture Readings

Acts 9:36-43; Psalm 23; Revelation 7:9-17; John 10:22-30

Theme Ideas

God is both the Good Shepherd and the holy and salvific Lamb. God's sheep know God's voice, and are called to love and serve God in many ways—creating beautiful things and serving others: As Tabitha did in Acts, with her sewing and charity to widows; resting in God's care beside streams and in lush pastures, as depicted by the psalmist; falling before the eternal throne and worshiping God forever, as in Revelation; and, following Jesus and getting to know his voice, as shown by John.

Invitation and Gathering

Contemporary Gathering Words (Psalm 23, John 10, Revelation 7)

> Come and worship! Sing your heart's song. Fall down
> before God's throne. Rest in fields of blessing and hope.
> Come and worship!

Call to Worship (Psalm 23, Revelation 7, John 10, Acts 9)

> Come and worship!
> **We are here, with God's Spirit among us.**
> God reveals God's self to us today:
> **As the Good Shepherd, giver of rest and comfort;**
> As the Holy Lamb, worthy of our eternal praise;
> **As the giver of new life, and new hope.**
> We are here, with God's Spirit among us.
> **We worship you, Holy Trinity.**

Opening Prayer (Acts 9, Psalm 23, Revelation 7:12a NRSV, John 10)

> Holy Lamb and Gentle Shepherd, we are here,
> the sheep of your pasture.
> Lead us in your ways.
> We come, from every nation and every language.
> We come, needing rest and wanting challenge.
> We come, kneeling in awe
> and standing in the promise of new life.
> We come with Peter, with Tabitha, with John,
> with the psalmist, and with the heavenly hosts,
> as we sing to you over and over:

"Blessing and glory and wisdom
and thanksgiving and honor...
be to our God forever!"
Bless this time of worship, Beautiful Savior,
and guide us to springs of your living water.

Proclamation and Response

Prayer of Confession (John 10, Acts 9)

Jesus our Lord, we ask for your forgiveness—
for what we have done, but shouldn't have,
for what we should have done, but didn't.
We yearn to hear your voice, Gentle Shepherd,
but listen to our own voices instead.
We want to care for our sisters and brothers,
to comfort them when they hurt,
to give what we have to people who have less,
but we choose to hoard our resources and time.
Forgive us, Lord, and help us forgive ourselves too
for everything we name before you now...
(Allow prayer to continue in silence.)
In your holy name, we pray. Amen.

Words of Assurance (John 10)

Children of God, hear these words of promise:
Christ our Shepherd joyfully welcomes us back
into the fold of love and freedom,
teaching us to know his voice.
In the name of Jesus the Christ, you are forgiven.
In the name of Jesus the Christ, you are forgiven.
Praise and thanks to God! Amen.

Passing the Peace of Christ (John 10)

As a forgiven and reconciled flock, take a moment to
spread the joy and peace of Christ with those around you!

Introduction to the Word or Prayer of Preparation (John 10)
>Listen! The voice of our Shepherd is calling.
>>**Speak, Lord, for we are your flock.**
>>**We know your voice and we are listening.**

Response to the Word (Revelation 7, Acts 9, Psalm 23, John 10)
>In the company of angels and heavenly elders,
>in the company of sisters and brothers who have come
>through the valley of the shadow of death
>and have seen resurrection in body or soul,
>>**we worship the One who wipes away our tears**
>>**and nourishes us with bread and living water.**
>We worship the Gentle Shepherd,
>who walks with us and calls us by name.
>>**We worship God the Invigorating Spirit,**
>>**who empowers us to "get up!" and come to life.**

Thanksgiving and Communion

Invitation to the Offering (Acts 9)
>We invite you to give your offerings with a joyful and generous heart. Whether you choose to offer gifts of money, prayer, talents, service, or witness, we encourage you to give as the Spirit leads. With Tabitha, in Acts, let us be devoted to seeking good and to doing charity together.

Offering Prayer (Revelation 7, John 10)
>Holy One, we give our gifts to you now,
>>knowing that you transform our earthly offerings
>>>into heavenly blessings.

May we desire to hear and know your voice,
     that we may worship you night and day,
          and fall down before your throne.
In your name, through the power of your Spirit,
     we pray together. Amen.

Sending Forth

Benediction (Acts 9, John 10, Revelation 7, Psalm 23)
     Go forth from this place, as disciples of the risen Christ,
          to love and serve your neighbor and your God.
     Go forth like Peter, Tabitha, and the disciples,
          to do good and charitable things,
          and to show others the wonder of our God,
          who is both Gentle Shepherd and Righteous Lamb.
     Go in peace and love!

April 24, 2016

Fifth Sunday of Easter
B. J. Beu

[Copyright © 2015 by B .J. Beu. Used by permission.]

Color

White

Scripture Readings

Acts 11:1-18; Psalm 148; Revelation 21:1-6; John 13:31-35

Theme Ideas

God draws no distinction between peoples, but loves all equally. Through a vision, Peter is shown that the Gentiles are to be included in the promises of God. The psalmist calls creation to praise the creator of heaven and earth. And Revelation promises that God will wipe away every tear, for God has come to dwell among us. Finally, in John's Gospel, Jesus commands disciples everywhere to love one another—for Christians will be known by their love.

Invitation and Gathering

Contemporary Gathering Words (Acts 11)
Visions disturb us in the night, depicting a world where God breaks down the barriers that separate us and keep

us apart—barriers that alienate us from one another and from ourselves. God's visions disturb our complacency. Thanks be to God.

Call to Worship (Acts 11, Psalm 148, Revelation 21, John 21)
The One who loves without distinction calls us here.
From the highest heavens to the deepest ravine,
let all creation praise the Lord.
The One who loves us calls us into God's future.
From the rising sun to the waning moon,
let all creation praise the Lord.
The One who loves us calls us still.
From the new heaven and new earth,
let all creation praise the Lord.

Opening Prayer (Revelation 21, John 13)
Wipe away our tears, O God,
for we are weary of weeping
at the injustices of the world.
Love us like a mother,
and protect us like a father,
that we may live as your beloved children
in a world made new.
Dwell among us, we pray,
that we may love one another
as we were meant to love. Amen

Proclamation and Response

Prayer of Confession (Acts 11, John 13)
Teach our hearts to love, O God,
as you would have us love.

Teach our eyes to see, Holy One,
    as you would have us see.
For we are constantly drawing distinctions,
    that separate others into friends and foes,
        insiders and outsiders.
You would have us love without prejudice.
You would have us accept without judgment.
You would have us truly learn to love.
Make your home among us,
    that we might be made one and whole. Amen.

Words of Assurance (Acts 11, Psalm 148, Revelation 21)
The One who made heaven and earth
    dwells among us to bring us love and life.
Let us Praise the Lord our God,
    for the One who loves us is faithful.

Passing the Peace of Christ (Acts 11)
Sometimes it takes a vision to see the world as God intends it to be. Share God's vision of unconditional welcome and love as we pass the peace of Christ.

Response to the Word (Acts 11, John 13)
The Spirit falls upon God's people without consideration of the prejudices of those who call themselves Christian. Such acceptance is unsettling to us. Yet it is the way of the gospel of love—a love we are commanded to share with one another. Thank God!

Thanksgiving and Communion

Invitation to the Offering (Revelation 21, John 13)
If we truly believe God dwells among us, would we live differently? Would we love differently? Would we give differently? Truly I tell you, God dwells among us even

now. Let us share our faith and our love accordingly, as
we collect this morning's offering.

Offering Prayer (Acts 11, John 13)
>God of mystery,
>>you promise us a life of blessedness,
>>>if we learn to love one another
>>>>as you have first loved us.
>May the gifts we offer you today,
>>be a sign of our commitment
>>>to see beyond our narrow perspective
>>>>as we learn to love one another
>>>>>with your all embracing vision.

Sending Forth

Benediction (John 13)
>A new commandment sends us forth...
>>**We are called to love one another.**
>A new vision guides our way...
>>**We are told to see God's acceptance,**
>>**even of the stranger.**
>A new blessing leads us forward...
>>**We are called to be a blessing to the world.**

May 1, 2016

Sixth Sunday of Easter
Leigh Anne Taylor

Color

White

Scripture Readings

Acts 16:9-15; Psalm 67; Revelation 21:1-10, 22–22:5; John 14:23-29

Theme Ideas

Today's readings remind us that Christian faith is about relationships: the believer living in God, and the triune God living with us and in us. When Lydia became a believer, she made a home in her heart for God, and she made room in her house for Paul and the disciples. As Jesus promised, the Holy Spirit lives in his followers, teaching and reminding them of all that he said. Nations who follow God's guidance will receive the saving power and blessing of God and be judged with justice and equity. The ultimate promise for all who live in God is consolation, healing, provision, and peace.

Invitation and Gathering

Contemporary Gathering Words (Psalm 67, Revelation 21, John 14)

What would your life be like if you made a home for the Holy Spirit in your heart and mind? What would our worship life be like if we made a home for the Holy Spirit in the heart and mind of our congregation? What would our world be like if the love and justice of God ruled in every nation? Let us imagine such a life and such a world as we worship the God who lives in us today.

Call to Worship (Psalm 67, Revelation 21, John 14)

Look! God is making a home among us!
**God, we welcome your justice and salvation
within us and between us.**
The Son of God is making our lives
the home of God's love and light.
**Jesus Christ, we welcome your love and light
within us and between us.**
The Spirit of God is making our hearts and lives
a home for God.
**Holy Spirit, we welcome your peace and guidance
within us and between us.**
Let us worship the triune God!
We welcome God home!

Opening Prayer (Acts 16, John 14)

Jesus, our Savior, you promised your disciples
that God would send the Holy Spirit in your name,
reminding them of your teachings
and leading them forward into new truths
yet to be revealed.

We have heard of the mighty acts of those
    who received the gift of your promised Holy Spirit,
        and we are amazed.
We dare to invite this same Holy Spirit into our lives,
    to teach us and to guide us,
        that we too may learn of God's love and justice.
By the grace and power of the Holy Spirit,
    may your word make a home in us today. Amen.

Proclamation and Response

Prayer of Confession (Psalm 67, Revelation 21)
Holy God,
you have made your living word known to us
    in the life, death, and resurrection
        of your Son Jesus,
        but we have failed to keep your word.
You have shown us how to live in your light,
    but we have chosen to dwell in darkness.
    **Without your mercy, we have no hope,
        no future, O God.**
You have shown us the way of peace,
    but we have chosen paths of greed, exploitation,
        and hostility between peoples and nations.
    **Without your mercy, we have no hope,
        no future, O God.**
You have shown us the way of salvation,
    but we have embraced practices that lead to death:
        Lying, idolatry, faithlessness, cowardice,
            sexual immorality, murder, drug abuse…
    **Without your mercy, we have no hope,
        no future, O God.**

Have mercy on us, according to your loving-kindness.
Forgive our sins and restore us by your grace,
>   that we may resist the powers of evil,
>   live in your light, and keep your word. Amen.

Words of Assurance (Psalm 67)
>   With justice and equity, God forgives everyone
>   who earnestly repents of their sin.
>   May God's face shine upon us and save us from our sin.
>   **Thanks be to God. Amen.**

Passing the Peace of Christ (John 14; see John 15:4)
>   Jesus said, "Live in me and I will live in you." As we
>   greet one another with the peace of Christ, rejoice that
>   Jesus Christ lives in each one of us.

Introduction to the Word or Prayer of Preparation (John 14)
>   Holy Spirit, make a way for the living word of God
>   to make a home in us today. Amen.
>   *(May lead into the song: "Into My Heart," v.1)*

Response to the Word (John 14)
>   By the grace of God, let us keep these words,
>   so that God will live in us. Amen.
>   *(May lead into the song: "Into My Heart," v.1)*

Thanksgiving and Communion

Invitation to the Offering (Acts 16)
>   *(May begin with the song: "Into My Heart," v.2)*
>   When Lydia became a believer and was baptized in the
>   faith, she invited Paul and his companions to stay in
>   her home. Generous giving naturally follows believing!
>   May our giving joyfully reflect our believing.

Offering Prayer (Psalm 67)
> Gracious God, we thank you for the abundant blessings
> > you bestow upon the earth.
> As we offer these gifts, in thanksgiving and praise,
> > we pray that they will be a blessing to others.
> Through our gifts, may the word of your goodness
> > spread to the ends of the earth,
> > > that all people may know of your love
> > > > and make a home for you in their hearts.
> > Amen.

Sending Forth

Benediction (Acts 16, Revelation 21, John 14)
> May your heart be a home for Christ.
> May your home be a place where God's love abounds.
> May your heart and your home so abide in God's love
> > that everyone who knows you will say,
> > "Look! God lives here!"

May 8, 2016

Ascension Sunday
Susan A. Blain

Color

White

Scripture Readings

Acts 1:1-11; Psalm 47; Ephesians 1:15-23; Luke 24:44-53

Theme Ideas

Ascension Day begins a period of waiting for the followers of Jesus. The risen Christ, who has been wonderfully and unexpectedly present with them since Easter—comforting, teaching, challenging—leaves them to return to the One who sent him into their midst in the first place. Christ leaves those early followers with many unanswered questions, but also with the promise that the Spirit will come to empower them for a future that they can hardly imagine. The time between Ascension Day and Pentecost is what we might call a "retreat." It is a time when the disciples gather together to wait and ponder all that has happened to them, and to prepare for this new moment in the mission they will share. "Why are you looking up to heaven?" is the challenge posed to the disciples by the two strangers in dazzling robes. The prayer, the work, the mission, the very Spirit of Christ is discovered here on earth, in new and surprising ways.

Invitation and Gathering

Contemporary Gathering Words (Acts 1, Luke 24)
Hoping to see where Jesus has gone, we look to the skies. Searching for God, we peer into the heavens. But God is nearer to us than our very breath. And Jesus is with us when we gather in his name. Look around you. Here is your God. Here is the one you love, the one you are looking for.
(B. J. Beu)

Call to Worship (Ephesians 1)
Mystery of God, draw us near.
    Fill our minds with awe!
Wisdom of God, surprise us.
    Encourage us with hope!
Glory of God, shine through our lives.
    Reveal your power and your glory!
In the mystery, the wisdom, the glory of God,
    Let us worship!

Opening Prayer (Acts 1)
Unknowable God, on this most unsettling day,
        you drew Jesus to your side—
            promising his companions Spirit, power,
                mission, and purpose;
            calling his disciples to trust a future
                that they could not yet see.

As we look to Jesus this day,
    give us the same hope of Spirit, power,
        mission and purpose,
            and call to trust a future
                that we too are yet unable to see.
Guide us into your depths,
    that we may glimpse the Spirit
        already at work in our lives—
            revealing your truth
                and empowering us to bear witness
                    to the risen Christ.
We pray this in the name of Jesus,
    your Mystery, your Wisdom, your Glory.

Proclamation and Response

Prayer of Confession (Acts 1, Luke 24:47-48)
    The story of Ascension Day challenges us to seek the
presence of the risen Christ in the here and now—in our
lives, our community, and our world. Let us pray.
When we "look up to heaven" for our answers,
and so fail to seek the Spirit at work in our midst—
    Lord, have mercy.
When we forget to repent of our wrong doings;
when we fail to forgive others for mistakes of their own,
and so fail to give witness to the risen Christ—
    Christ, have mercy.
When we doubt the power of your Spirit,
which is at work changing hearts and opening minds,
and so fail to embrace relationships
of righteousness and peace—
    Lord have mercy.

Words of Assurance
Friends, the love of God revealed in Jesus
forgives us, heals us, and sets us free
to witness to his love in the world.

Passing the Peace of Christ (Ephesians 1:15-16a)
In the spirit of Paul, who gave thanks for the community's faith in the risen Christ and for their love for one
another, let us pass the peace of Christ.

Scripture Ritual
*(The Christ Candle, symbol of the risen Christ, is traditional-
ly processed out of the sanctuary following the reading of the
Ascension Day Gospel. This startling and unsettling ritual
makes the point that Jesus must now be present to us in a new
way. Have a worship leader bring the Pascal Candle into the
center of the congregation as the Gospel is read, then continue
its journey out of the sanctuary after the reading)*

Introduction to the Word (Psalm 47:5-6, Inclusive Bible)
(As the Christ Candle is taken into the congregation)
God ascended the throne with a shout,
with trumpet blasts!
Sing praises to God, sing praises.
Sing praises to our ruler, sing praises!

Response to the Word (Acts 1: 10-11a NRSV)
(After the Christ Candle has been taken out)
As Jesus was going, the disciples gazed toward heaven,
when suddenly two strangers in white robes
stood by them, saying:
"Why do you stand looking up toward heaven?"

Thanksgiving and Communion

Invitation to the Offering (Luke 24:47)

Christ calls us to participate in a mission of reconciliation throughout the world—inviting us to participate in the building up of the body of Christ, where justice and peace prevail. Let us give generously of our time, talents, and treasure to foster this mission.

Offering Prayer

O God, we bring to you this offering,
    and ask you to bless it and use it
        to make your reign known in our world.
In Jesus' name, we pray. Amen.

Sending Forth

Benediction (Acts 1, Luke 24:53)

The disciples looked up to heaven,
    and then looked around at each other.
Slowly, understanding dawned upon them
    as they began to recognize the presence
    of their beloved Jesus in their midst.
With their minds enlightened, and their hearts set free,
    they went forth rejoicing, singing and praying,
    and waiting for the Spirit's coming.
Let us, too, go forth confident in God.
Let us rejoice in one another,
    as we wait in prayer for the surprise of the Spirit.
—Or—

Benediction (Ephesians 1:17-19 Inclusive Bible)

"I pray that the God of our Savior Jesus Christ, the God of glory, will give you a spirit of wisdom and revelation, to bring you to a rich knowledge of the Creator.... [May] God...enlighten the eyes of your mind so that you can see the hope this call holds for you—the promised glories that God's Holy Ones will inherit, and the infinitely great power that is exercised for us who believe."

May 15, 2016

Pentecost Sunday
Safiyah Fosua

Color

Red

Scripture Readings

Acts 2:1-21; Psalm 104:24-34, 35b; Romans 8:14-17;
John 14:8-17 (25-27)

Theme Ideas

Festival days in the Christian calendar are often more
challenging than those in ordinary time because they
have become familiar to the congregation and worship
planners. In spite of the liturgical challenges, Pentecost
remains one of the most significant holy days of the
Christian calendar because it dramatizes how the children of God (Romans 8:14-17), emerged with the power needed to do the greater works that Jesus promised
(John 14:8-17). The familiar text from Acts 2 reminds
us of the highly inclusive nature of God's holy Church
from the time that it sprang into existence. From the day
that the Church became visible, we are reminded that
our mission as the body of Christ is to reach those who

have not had an opportunity to hear God in a language
that they understand.

Invitation and Gathering

Contemporary Gathering Words (Romans 8:14 NRSV)
Come.
Come closer.
Draw near.
Whether in shalom or weariness…
In want or in plenty…
In certainty or in questioning…
You are welcome!
Come closer.
Draw near.
God is calling us together.
"For all who are led by the Spirit of God
are children of God."

Call to Worship (Acts 2)
Like the ancient followers
who waited for days in an upstairs, prayer room,
we wait before God.
And though we wait in faith,
we are not certain how God will come to us.
And yet we wait,
certain that the wait is worthwhile.
For, those who waited long ago
received an outpouring of God's promised Spirit.
And so, in faith, we have come to wait
before God!

Opening Prayer (Acts 2, Romans 8)
Loving God, you have led each of us here today.
Though most of us have heard the story of Pentecost,

restore in us the ability to perceive the wonder
and the awe of the outpouring of your Spirit
upon humankind long ago.
Help us hear this familiar story with new ears,
that we might depart from this place
with newly discovered zeal,
declaring that you are alive in us,
your body, the Church. Amen.

Proclamation and Response

Prayer of Confession (Acts 2)
God of wind and flame,
as we bow before you on this Pentecost Sunday,
we confess to being distracted by this day.
Our preoccupation with new ways to use the color red
threatens to overshadow the awe and glory
inspired by your ancient texts.
God of amazement and wonder,
we need a vision of Pentecost
that is bigger than fan-driven streamers,
red flowers, and banners of fire.
Remind us how your Spirit breaks across barriers
of language and racial origins,
reaching out to people
who have been unable to understand you.
Remind us once more,
that you use us to communicate
with those who are different from ourselves.
Set our hearts on fire this day, as you did long ago.
Spill us out into the streets,
with your words in our mouths,

that our motley world might know your Spirit
and be healed. Amen.

Words of Assurance (Romans 8)
The same God who has adopted us
and called us children and heirs,
hears our heartfelt confession and pardons us
from all unrighteousness.
In the name of Jesus Christ, you are forgiven.

Response to the Word (Acts 2)
Wind of God,
blow again!
Tongues of Fire,
burn again!
Spirit of God,
pour over us again,
and send us into the streets
to proclaim your glory!

Thanksgiving and Communion

Offering Prayer (John 14:8-17)
Gracious and loving God,
Christ promised that those who believe in you
will do the works that he did.
We have gathered in this congregation
to worship you, and to serve you,
and to serve the ministries you have given us
in support of our community and the world.
Receive our humble offerings as our spiritual worship.
May our gifts be used for your glory,
as we look toward doing the greater works

you promised that we would do
in your name. Amen.

Sending Forth

Benediction
May you be transformed by the fires of Pentecost
that began to burn more than two millennia ago.
May you be encouraged, emboldened, and empowered
by God's Spirit to leave the safety of your hiding place.
And may you be given the courage to bear
any consequences of speaking the words of healing
that come from God.
We leave the safety of this upper room—
willing to be transformed,
willing to risk being misunderstood or ridiculed,
claiming the power of the Holy Spirit
to make a difference in the world. Amen.

May 22, 2016

Trinity Sunday
Mary J. Scifres

Color

White

Scripture Readings

Proverbs 8:1-4, 22-31; Psalm 8; Romans 5:1-5;
John 16:12-15

Theme Ideas

On this Trinity Sunday, the Spirit of Wisdom emerges as
a primary theme. Created in the beginning, the Spirit of
Wisdom rejoices in God's creation and brings truth and
wisdom to the human creature. Sent as a gift after Jesus'
Ascension, this Spirit inspires and empowers Christ's
followers to live the truth we have received from Christ.

Invitation and Gathering

Contemporary Gathering Words (Proverbs 8, Romans 5)
Wisdom cries out to us. The Spirit is here, blowing where
she will and strengthening our journey of faith.

Call to Worship (Proverbs 8, John 16)
The Spirit of God is here,
calling us to worship and praise.
The Spirit delights in our presence,
rejoicing alongside us.
The Spirit of Truth is still speaking,
granting wisdom for our lives today.

Opening Prayer (Proverbs 8, Romans 5)
Spirit of God, breathe your wisdom
into our thoughts this day.
Inspire and strengthen us,
that we may be people of faith and hope.
In your Holy Spirit, we pray.

Proclamation and Response

Prayer of Confession (Proverbs 8, Romans 5, John 16)
Spirit of Wisdom and Truth,
open our ears to hear your cry;
broaden our minds to understand your truth;
strengthen our hearts to trust your ways.
Forgive us when we cling to old habits
that keep us from embracing fullness of life—
when we hide from your presence;
when we ignore your guidance;
when we avoid your direction.
Restore us and renew us,
that we may again hear and respond
as you blow through our lives.

Words of Assurance (John 16)
The Spirit of Truth guides us and renews us.

The grace of Christ Jesus reconciles us to God,
  our creator, who forgives us and makes us whole.
Rejoice in the truth of God's love!

Passing the Peace of Christ (Proverbs 8)
  Just as God rejoices in us, and God's Holy Spirit delights
  in our presence, so may we delight in one another. Share
  signs of joy and love as we pass the peace of Christ.

Introduction to the Word (Proverbs 8, John 16)
  The Spirit of Truth is here to grant us wisdom and offer
  us hope. Listen, for the Spirit is still speaking.

Response to the Word (Proverbs 8, John 16)
  Wisdom calls.
    We are listening.
  The Spirit speaks.
    We have heard her!
  Truth will guide us.
    We will follow the Spirit of Truth.

Thanksgiving and Communion

Offering Prayer (Proverbs 8, Psalm 8)
  Thank you, Holy Spirit,
    for delighting in creation
      and inspiring us with your gifts.
  As we share these gifts of joy and love
    with Christ's holy church,
      bless these gifts with your presence,
        that they may bring your hope and wisdom
          to God's beautiful, created world.

Sending Forth

Benediction (Proverbs 8, John 16)
Empowered by the Holy Spirit,
we go forth in hope and faith.
Inspired by the Spirit of Truth,
we go forth with God's wisdom and love.

May 29, 2016

Second Sunday after Pentecost, Proper 4
B. J. Beu

Color

Green

Scripture Readings

1 Kings 18:20-21, (22-29), 30-39; Psalm 96;
Galatians 1:1-12; Luke 7:1-10

Theme Ideas

When it comes to worshiping God in the manner we have received, is it all or nothing? Elijah chastises the Israelites for following Ba'al and rejecting the Lord. The psalmist claims that the Lord is to be revered above all gods. Paul is astonished that the Galatians have so quickly deserted the One who called them in the grace of Christ, by accepting a perverted gospel. Jesus heals the servant of a Roman centurion and marvels at the soldier's faith—a faith greater than any he found in Israel. These texts suggest that when it comes to the purity of our faith and gospel, no compromises are allowed. This is surely true if we are worshiping Ba'al or a perverted form of the gospel of Christ—but what do we tell people who practice Buddhist meditation and compassion, or who hold Native Peoples' beliefs that Spirit animates all things? Some lines must be held at all costs, as in the case of Elijah. But during a time when Christian, Zionist, and Islamic fundamentalists are tearing the social fabric of our world apart, are we wise to insist that our tradition alone is faithful?

Invitation and Gathering

Contemporary Gathering Words (1 Kings 18, Psalm 96, Luke 7)
> The sick are healed. The weak are strengthened. The truth is revealed in glorious power. The stories of our faith shape us, and guide us. They orient us, and help us keep our bearings. They witness the conviction of prophets and apostles, the certainty of those from whom we would least expect it. These are stories of hope and salvation. These are our stories.

Call to Worship (Psalm 96)
> Sing to the Lord a new song.
> > **Let the heavens be glad,**
> > **and the earth rejoice.**
> Sing to the Lord a song of praise.
> > **Let the mountains quake,**
> > **and the seas roar.**
> Sing to the Lord a song of hope.
> > **Let us tell of God's salvation**
> > **and the greatness of God's love.**

Opening Prayer (1 Kings 18, Psalm 96)
> God of heaven and earth,
> > we sing your praises
> > > with the trees of the forest;

we proclaim your might
with the roaring of the seas.
As we gather this day for worship—
hear our prayers,
heed our cries,
sustain our faith,
and calm our fears.
Bless the earth with righteousness,
and your peoples with truth,
that we may walk blamelessly before you,
all the days of our lives. Amen.

Proclamation and Response

Prayer of Confession (1 Kings 18, Psalm 96, Galatians 1, Luke 7)
God of power and glory,
voices are all around us,
telling us what you expect of us
and how we should live our lives,
but we're not sure who to listen to.
Should we listen to voices of exclusion,
telling us to reject other spiritual paths
if we are to be Christ's disciples
and know the glory of your salvation?
Or should we listen to voices of inclusion,
inviting us embrace spiritual practices
of compassion and mercy,
where ever they are found,
even as we strive to be faithful followers
of Jesus Christ?

In matters of faith,
    we long for the bravado of Elijah,
        the conviction of Paul,
            and the certainty of the Roman centurion,
    but we often find ourselves in uncharted seas—
        yearning for a guide
            who truly knows those waters.
Speak to us now in the quiet center of our hearts,
    that we may see your ways more clearly,
        and taste the sweetness of your truth and grace.
    Amen.

Words of Assurance (Psalm 96, Galatians 1, Luke 7)
There is only one true gospel of Jesus Christ—
    it is a gospel of righteousness,
    a gospel that embraces all people,
    a gospel of forgiveness, reconciliation, and love.
Christ's gospel is always bigger, more inclusive,
    and more wonderful,
    than we could possibly dream.
Thanks be to God!

Passing the Peace of Christ (Galatians 1, Colossians 3)
In a world where people hate and kill one another in the name of their gods, let us proclaim the God we know and worship, as we share signs of love and peace.

Prayer of Preparation (1 Kings 18)
Holy, holy, holy Lord,
    open our hearts and minds
        to receive your word of truth this day.
Send the fire of your Spirit,
    to lead us in wisdom and understanding,
        that we may live your gospel of love. Amen.

Response to the Word *(1 Kings 18, Psalm 96, Galatians 1, Luke 7:9 NRSV)*

> We live is a world of uncertainty, O God.
> Bless us with the bravado of Elijah,
> > the conviction of Paul,
> > > and the certainty of the Roman centurion,
> > > > that Jesus may look at us and exclaim:
> > > > > "Not even in Israel
> > > > > > have I found such faith."

Thanksgiving and Communion

Offering Prayer *(1 Kings 18, Psalm 96)*

> You rain the fire of your Holy Spirit
> > upon our lives, O God,
> > > demonstrating the power of your love.
> You bless us with a world of wonder and delight—
> > a world where trees sing your praises,
> > > and seas roar your glory.
> In awe and gratitude for the blessings in our lives,
> > we offer these gifts back to you,
> > > as signs of our love and faithfulness. Amen.

Sending Forth

Benediction *(1 Kings 18, Psalm 96, Luke 7)*

> With visions of God's holy fire
> raining down from heaven,
> > **we go forth with awe in our hearts.**
> With dreams of trees singing God's praise
> and seas roaring God's glory,
> > **we go forth with wonder and amazement.**
> With stories of faith and hope
> bringing healing and new life,
> > **we go forth with peace and joy.**

June 5, 2016

Third Sunday after Pentecost, Proper 5
B. J. Beu

Color

Green

Scripture Readings

1 Kings 17:8-24; Psalm 146; Galatians 1:11-24;
Luke 7:11-17

Theme Ideas

Today's scriptures proclaim new life in situations of death. In 1 Kings, Elijah transforms empty jars and lamps into an abundant supply of grain and light, then brings a widow's son back from the brink of death. In Luke, Jesus comforts a grieving mother, then brings her son back from the dead. Both Elijah and Jesus are seen as messengers of the God who watches over widows and provides food to the hungry. In Galatians, Paul moves from spiritual death to life, as he is transformed from one who persecuted the church to an apostle who proclaims the good news of life in Christ.

Invitation and Gathering

Contemporary Gathering Words (1 Kings 17, Psalm 146, Luke 7)

Jars of meal that do not empty...Jugs of lamp oil that do not fail...Persecutors of the church transformed into apostles of Christ. Children brought back from the dead...Is anything impossible for our God? Let us worship the Lord—who watches over the stranger, upholds the orphan and the widow, and executes justice for the poor.

Call to Worship (Psalm 146)

Sing praises to the Lord, sing praises.
We will praise the Lord as long as we live!
God executes justice for the oppressed
and gives food to the hungry.
God opens the eyes of the blind
and lifts up the weary.
God watches over the stranger
and upholds the orphan and the widow,
but the evil and the wicked
are brought to ruin.
Sing praises to the Lord, sing praises.
We will praise the Lord as long as we live!

Opening Prayer (1 Kings 17, Psalm 146, Galatians 1, Luke 7)

God of help and hope,
your miracles are a constant presence in our lives.
Though we look for the jar of grain that doesn't empty
and the jug of oil the doesn't fail,
you surprise us with everyday miracles—

justice for the poor and oppressed,
care of the orphan and the widow,
the downfall of the haughty and the proud.
Lift us up and dry our tears,
when breath leaves the body of those we love.
Train our eyes to see hope and new life all around us,
that we may walk in faith
as followers of your Son. Amen.

Proclamation and Response

Prayer of Confession (1 Kings 17, Psalm 146, Luke 7)
Merciful God,
in our struggle to simply get through the day,
we have lost the passion of your calling.
When we neglect to care
for the widow and the orphan,
the stranger and those who are lost,
forgive us.
When we fail to stop and take notice
of the glory of your creation
and the wonder of your handiwork,
open our eyes once more.
Breathe new life into our weary bodies,
and call us back from the brink of death,
that we may joyfully proclaim
the gospel of your love and peace. Amen.

Words of Assurance (Psalm 146, Galatians 1, Luke 7)
Happy are those whose help is in the Lord,
whose hope is in the God of our friend and savior,
Christ Jesus.
God calls us to be happy, forgiven, and free. Amen.

Passing the Peace of Christ (1 Kings 17, Luke 7)
The power of God fills jars with grain and jugs with oil.
The power of God brings the dead back to live. Let us
give thanks for the miracles of God, by sharing signs of
joy and peace with one another.

*Response to the Word or Benediction (1 Kings 17, Galatians
1, Luke 7)*
God invites us on new journeys of faith.
God gives us courage to answer the call.
God fills the empty vessels of our lives
with grain and oil to spare.
God blesses our lives with bread and light.
God breathes new life into places of death.
God opens our hearts to receive the Holy Spirit.
Walk this journey of faith.
We will walk with our God.

Thanksgiving and Communion

Invitation to the Offering (1 Kings 17)
Do not fear famine or want. God's gifts overflow in our
lives. Our jars will not fail. Our cups will not empty. Do
not be afraid, but believe. Let us give generously as we
collect today's offering, for God has given generously
to us.

Offering Prayer (1 Kings 17, Luke 7)
God of overflowing abundance,
    you fill the empty jars of our lives
        with life-giving grain
            to nourish our bodies;
    you fill the dried out vessels of our spirit

with light-giving oil
　　to illumine our path.
Receive these gifts, in thanksgiving and praise
　　for your love and mercy,
　　　　that others may know your abundant grace.
Amen.

Communion Prayer (1 Kings 17, Galatians 1)
Pour out your Holy Spirit,
　　on these gifts of bread and wine,
　　　　that they may be for us
　　　　　　vessels of light and love,
　　　　　　　　joy and hope.
Walk with us in the power of your Spirit,
　　that we might be one with Christ,
　　　　one with each other,
　　　　　　and one in ministry to the world.
Strengthen us until Christ comes in final victory
　　and we feast with him at your heavenly banquet.
Amen.
(Mary J. Scifres and B. J. Beu)

Giving the Bread and Cup
(The bread and wine are given to the people, with these or other words of blessing.)
The life of Christ, revealed in you.
The love of Christ, flowing through you.
(Mary J. Scifres)

Sending Forth

Benediction (1 Kings 17, Galatians 1, Psalm 146)
Go with God's grace to serve the world.
We will go where God sends us.

Work for justice and righteousness for all.
We go to serve God's people.
Bring healing, hope, and new life wherever you go.
We go as disciples of Christ.

June 12, 2016

Fourth Sunday after Pentecost, Proper 6
Mary J. Scifres

Color

Green

Scripture Readings

1 Kings 21:1-21a; Psalm 5:1-8; Galatians 2:15-21;
Luke 7:36–8:3

Theme Ideas

In today's readings, two infamous women are front and center: Jezebel and the sinful woman who bathed Jesus' feet with her tears. The power of stereotypes challenges us in these passages: Simon the Pharisee struggled with prejudice when he judged the woman who was anointing Jesus; and Paul struggled to accept and include Gentiles in the early church, reminding himself and others that grace is the common link between followers of Christ. King Ahab and Jezebel seem almost caricatures of self-absorbed, evil rulers. One could easily see Darth Vader of Star Wars and the White Witch of Narnia playing their roles. But even in basic stories of good versus evil, the human need for grace abides. Heroes fall short, and villains have a chance at redemption. This is not a fictional theme, but the theme of our human experience. Sinful women become the first to worship and anoint Jesus, and murderous inquisitors become transformed into leaders of the church, just as Saul was transformed into Paul. Grace is indeed amazing in its power to transform.

Invitation and Gathering

Contemporary Gathering Words (Psalm 5, Galatians 2)
God's abundant love invites us here. Christ's loving grace welcomes all. Come, the Spirit gathers us as one!

Call to Worship (Psalm 5)
God is here,
> **filling us with love and joy.**

God is here,
> **guiding our steps.**

We are here,
> **ready to worship and sing.**

(This Call to Worship leads easily into the hymn, "God Is Here.")

Opening Prayer (Luke 7)
Holy God, pour out your holiness on us.
Pour out your strength,
> that we may worship you
>> with the confidence of beloved children.

Pour out your grace,
> that we may enter your presence,
>> fully and completely,
>>> loving you with our tears, our prayers,

and our praise.
In love and gratitude, we pray. Amen.

Proclamation and Response

Prayer of Confession (Psalm 5, Luke 7)
Welcome us, gracious God,
as Jesus welcomed sinners and saints alike.
Forgive the wrongs we have done,
and the acts of mercy we have left undone.
Bless us with your mercy and grace,
especially when we feel friendless
and beaten down.
Reassure us of your love,
especially when we feel most alone
and most undeserving.
Welcome us into your holy presence
with forgiving grace and faithful love
that never ends.
In Christ's name, we pray. Amen.

Words of Assurance (Luke 7)
In the love of Christ, your sins are forgiven.
In the love of Christ, your sins are forgiven!
Praise God for this glorious gift!

Passing the Peace of Christ (Luke 7)
Welcome one another with grace and love, for all are
welcome here!

Prayer of Preparation (Psalm 5)
Lead us, Lord.
Make your way clear.

Make your words plain,
that we might walk in your ways
and live in your love. Amen.

Response to the Word or Invitation to Anointing and Healing

Christ's love knows no limits.
All are welcome here.
Christ's grace is more powerful than our greatest fears.
All are welcome here.
Come to Christ, whose healing mercy
soothes the soul and strengthens the spirit.

Thanksgiving and Communion

Invitation to the Offering (Luke 7)

Bring your need and bathe Christ with your tears. Bring
your abundance and bless the world with your gifts. All
offerings that come from the heart are welcome. We all
have much to offer. Together, we have all that is needed.

Offering Prayer (Luke 7)

Gracious God, as you have anointed and healed us,
send these gifts forth to anoint and heal others.
Search out those who have lost their way,
yet yearn to worship you with their tears.
Help them discover just how much your love is theirs.
Strengthen our ministries and our lives,
that we may confidently kneel at your feet
with all who seek your holy presence.
Send us into your world to anoint and heal others,
as you have anointed and healed us.
In Christ's name, we pray. Amen.

Sending Forth

Benediction (Luke 7)
Your faith has saved you.
God's love has healed you.
Go in the peace of Christ.

June 19, 2016

Fifth Sunday after Pentecost, Proper 7
Father's Day

Mary J. Scifres

Color

Green

Scripture Readings

1 Kings 19:1-15a; Psalm 42; Galatians 3:23-29;
Luke 8:26-39

Theme Ideas

When faith casts out fear with the strength of God's
love, all things are possible. Elijah knew fear, but redis-
covered both his faith and his calling when he listened
for the voice of God. The people surrounding the Ger-
asenes knew fear, but they chased Jesus away instead
of listening for this new voice of hope and faith in their
midst. The man possessed by the demons named Le-
gion knew fear, but found faith in the dramatic healing
that Jesus offered. When faith met fear, both Elijah and
the man Jesus healed were sent forth to share their faith
and God's hope. The psalmist reminds us to speak faith

even to our inner fears: "Why, I ask myself, / are you so depressed? / Why are you upset inside? / Hope in God! / Because I will again give [God] thanks, / my saving presence and my God" (v. 5).

Invitation and Gathering

Contemporary Gathering Words (1 Kings 19, Psalm 42)
Faith calls us here, inviting us to leave our fears at the door. Enter into this time of worship with hope and trust in the God who loves us.

Call to Worship (1 Kings 19, Psalm 42)
Bring your longing, bring your hope.
God is with us here.
Lay down your fears, lay aside your doubts.
Faith has called us here.
Pour out your soul with prayer and praise.
We come to worship God.
—Or—

Call to Worship or Response to the Word (1 Kings 19, Psalm 42)
When tears are our food,
God comes with a feast.
When fear is our path,
God brings us courage.
When sorrow is our friend,
God comforts and loves us.
When all hope seems lost,
God is our rock and redeemer.

Opening Prayer (1 Kings 19, Psalm 42)

Come to us in silence and word, O God.
Speak to our hearts,
>   that we may hear and respond.
Soothe our souls,
>   that we may rest and renew.
Strengthen our spirits,
>   that we may grow in faith and courage.
In Christ's name, we pray. Amen.

Proclamation and Response

Prayer of Confession (1 Kings 19, Luke 8)
>   God of strength and courage,
>>   you know our every fear.
>   You know every demon that haunts our lives.
>   Heal us.
>   Strengthen us.
>   Forgive us.
>   Renew us.
>   By the power of your Holy Spirit,
>>   make us people of faith and hope.
>   In Christ's holy name, we pray.

Words of Assurance (Luke 8)
>   In the power of Christ, we are healed.
>   In the grace of God, we are forgiven.
>   Thanks be to God!
>   *—Or—*

Words of Assurance (Psalm 42)
> Hope in God.
> Trust in Christ's grace.
> Forgiveness is ours this day!

Passing the Peace of Christ (1 Kings 19, Galatians 3)
> Let us share signs of faith and joy with one another, that we may overcome the fears that prevent us from experiencing God's peace.
> May the peace of God be with you.
> **And also with you!**

Introduction to the Word (1 Kings 19)
> God is in our midst—not in a mighty wind, not in earthquake and fire, but in the silence of prayer, and in the reading of God's holy word.
> *—Or—*

Introduction to the Word (Psalm 42)
> As a deer needs the sustenance of flowing streams, we need the nourishment of God's guiding presence. Here and now, we will be sustained and nourished by God's holy word.

Prayer of Preparation (Psalm 42)
> Our whole being craves you, God.
> We thirst for your word
> > and long for your touch.
> Reveal your presence to us,
> > as we hear your message
> > > and meditate on your ways.

Response to the Word (1 Kings 19, Luke 8)
> Winds may buffet us,
> and storms may threaten...
> **but God's love endures.**

Earthquakes may shake us,
and the ground beneath us may rumble...
  but Christ is our sure foundation.
Sorrows may tear our hearts,
and fears may send us running...
  but the Spirit runs with us
  and strengthens us for the journey.
May faith be a friend that casts out fear,
freeing us to love and to live with joy!

Thanksgiving and Communion

Offering Prayer (1 Kings 19, Luke 8)
  We thank and praise you, O God,
      for the power of your healing touch
          and the gift of your saving presence.
  Bless these gifts,
      that they may bring the power of your gifts
          to a world in need.
  In Christ's mighty name, we pray.
  —Or—

Offering Prayer (1 Kings 19, Psalm 42, Luke 8)
  Mighty God, strengthen our gifts
      with the power of your Holy Spirit.
  May they become instruments of faith and love
      to cast out our fears,
          bringing joy and hope to your world.

Invitation to Communion (1 Kings 19)
God's angels have come to prepare this feast: Bread for the journey, refreshment for the soul. Come to the table, where love casts out fear, and grace welcomes all.

Sending Forth

Benediction (1 Kings 19, Psalm 42, Luke 8)
Go forth in the power of the Holy Spirit,
filled with faith and hope.
**We go forth in the love of God
to proclaim the miracles of Christ.**

June 26, 2016

Sixth Study after Pentecost, Proper 8
Amy B. Hunter

Color

Green

Scripture Readings

2 Kings 2:1-2, 6-14; Psalm 77:1-2, 11-20;
Galatians 5:1, 13-25; Luke 9:51-62

Theme Ideas

It is both costly and rewarding to keep company with Jesus as he turns toward Jerusalem. His deliberate choice means facing conflict, rejection, condemnation, and death. Luke's Gospel identifies this choice, not as Jesus' passion, but as his ascension. Called to follow Jesus on this journey, we may see these passages as a test: Don't be like the casual hangers-on who weren't fit to follow Jesus, but be as faithful and tenacious as Elisha. But as Christians, we can take heart, remembering that Jesus' closest friends and disciples failed him on his journey toward Jerusalem, the cross, and his ascension. It was not their steadfast loyalty but Jesus' resurrection that made them successors in his mission, and that called them, and us, to be his Church.

Invitation and Gathering

Contemporary Gathering Words (2 Kings 2, Psalm 77, Galatians 5, Luke 9)

There are times when the wind of God shakes everything we hold dear. Times change and leaders leave us. Our days fill up with troubles. Then we fall in love with Jesus, who sets us free, only to discover he is determined to go to the cross. Beloved, the wind of God indeed shakes everything we hold dear. But Jesus shows us that God's holy tempest carries everything back to the heart of our God.

Call to Worship (2 Kings 2, Galatians 5, Luke 9)

Taken up to heaven, Christ sets us truly free.

**Jesus, give us the power to be servants
of your love!**

Taken up to heaven, Christ asks us what we truly want.

**Jesus, give us the power to be servants
of your love!**

Taken up to heaven, Christ offers us God's Kingdom.

**Jesus, give us the power to be servants
of your love!**

Opening Prayer (2 Kings 2, Luke 9)

Determined God, you ask much more of us
than our superficial affection.
You challenge us to walk beside you
and to be your loyal companions,
witnessing your glory
and carrying on your mission.
Give us the faithfulness of Elisha,
who stayed with his master Elijah
until the very end.

And when our faith falls short,
help us rely on Jesus' faith.
Even when his followers betrayed him,
he remained faithful until the end,
even unto the cross.
May we share the grace of his resurrection,
and share in his victory and eternal life. Amen.

Proclamation and Response

Prayer of Confession (2 Kings 2, Luke 9)
Challenging God, we need you,
if we are to be the people you call us to be.
You invite us to be your body, the Church,
**but we beg you to give the mantle of discipleship
to someone else.**
You ask us to be hospitable to all we meet,
**but we urge you to rain disaster
on those we call our enemies.**
You ask us to be your beloved family and friends,
**but we want to know who we'll be stuck with
at parties and picnics.**
Forgive us, God, for being such poor company.
**Forgive us for treating your call
as a do-it-yourself project.**
Challenging God, we are lost without your grace—
**a grace that enables us to answer your call
and to serve lovingly in your kingdom. Amen.**

Words of Assurance (Galatians 5)
People of God, Jesus Christ has set us free!
In his love, we are truly free!

Blessed by God's forgiveness and grace,
>we walk with the Spirit in newness of life.

Passing the Peace of Christ (Galatians 5)
God's Spirit has given us life. Let us follow the Spirit, and greet one another with the life-giving peace of Jesus Christ.

Introduction to the Word (Psalm 77)
Let us open our ears, our minds, and our hearts, as we listen to the mighty deeds of God in scripture this morning.

Response to the Word (Luke 9)
God, you have spoken to us through your word.
>**Jesus, help us leave the busyness of our lives**
>>**to tell the world about God's kingdom.**
>**Teach us to keep looking forward**
>>**into fullness of life in your kingdom. Amen.**

Thanksgiving and Communion

Invitation to the Offering (Galatians 5:1, 13-25)
God's Spirit makes us faithful and generous people— people who belong to Jesus Christ. By our giving and our gifts, let us show our gratitude to God for the love we have received.

Offering Prayer (2 Kings 2, Psalm 77, Galatians 5, Luke 9)
God, receive our gifts,
>and transform them by your love
>>into the means to show forth your kingdom
>>>in this world.
—Or—

Offering Prayer (2 Kings 2, Galatians 5)
You always give us the freedom to turn back, O Lord,
    to take an easier road.
But when we have the strength to carry on
    and ask for a double portion of your Spirit,
        as Elisha before us,
            we find blessing upon blessing.
May these gifts reflect our gratitude
    for your many gifts,
        especially the fruit of your Spirit.
May these gifts lift up others in their need,
    that they may see their own freedom
        to turn and choose life. Amen.
(B. J. Beu)

Sending Forth

Benediction (2 Kings 2, Galatians 5, Luke 9)
Beloved, the wind of God
    shakes everything we hold dear.
May God give you strong hearts
    to remain as faithful as Elisha,
    who saw Elijah carried up to heaven.
May God's Holy Spirit fill your lives
    with the gift of God's presence.
And may you learn to trust Jesus,
    who reminds us in his ascension
    that God's holy tempest carries everything back
    to the heart of our God.

July 3, 2016

Seventh Sunday after Pentecost, Proper 9
B. J. Beu
[Copyright © 2015 by B. J. Beu. Used by permission.]

Color

Green

Scripture Readings

2 Kings 5:1-14; Psalm 30; Galatians 6:(1-6) 7-16;
Luke 10:1-11, 16-20

Theme Ideas

In 2 Kings, a young captive taken from her homeland entreats her master, Naaman, to travel to Israel and be healed of his leprosy. Another foreign servant convinces Naaman to do as the prophet Elisha bids, that Naaman may indeed be made clean. In Luke's Gospel, Jesus sends seventy followers out to share God's blessings and peace, knowing he is sending them out "as lambs among wolves" (v. 3). Galatians urges us to correct transgressors in a spirit of gentleness. True power, godly power, seems to come from those who have every reason to withhold it. God is there to save us, yet works through the most unexpected sources.

Invitation and Gathering

Contemporary Gathering Words (Galatians 6, Luke 10)
> God is speaking. Can we hear it? Do we perceive it? Are we even listening? God is speaking to us and through us. God is speaking, offering us healing and peace.

Call to Worship (Psalm 30, Luke 10)
> Sing praises to the Lord, sing praises.
> **We come to worship God with shouts of joy.**
> Sing praises to the Lord, sing praises.
> **We come to entreat Christ to turn our mourning into dancing.**
> Sing praises to the Lord, sing praises.
> **We come to touch the healing Spirit of God.**

Opening Prayer (2 Kings 5, Galatians 6, Luke 10)
> Merciful God, your ways are a mystery to us.
> You warn us of the strangers' ways,
>> then you bring us healing and peace
>>> through those we are taught to mistrust.
> You speak words of wisdom
>> through those we do not wish to hear.
> Bathe us in the healing waters of your love once more,
>> that we may be washed clean
>>> of our arrogance and presumption.
> Then send us forth with messages of peace,
>> that others may hear our words,
>>> and know that you are speaking still. Amen.

Proclamation and Response

Prayer of Confession (2 Kings 5, Psalm 30, Galatians 6, Luke 10:19)
Mysterious One,
you turn our mourning into dancing,
only to send us forth to proclaim your peace
like lambs into the midst of wolves;
you turn our weeping into shouts of joy,
only to call us to seek the welfare of those
who have abused and betrayed us;
you turn our scarcity into overflowing abundance,
only to instruct us to leave it all behind
and seek those who have gone astray.
You make us question our deeply held assumptions
and our unchallenged convictions.
As we seek to love those who have wounded us,
speak again the words Christ shared
with his disciples:
"Nothing will harm you."
Help us follow your ways,
that we all may be healed and made whole
as we work in your fields. Amen.

Words of Assurance (Psalm 30, Luke 10)
God's anger may last a moment,
but God's favor lasts a lifetime.
Weeping may last the night,
but joy comes in the morning.
Rejoice and be glad,
for our names are written in heaven.

Passing the Peace of Christ (Luke 10)
Jesus sent his disciples forth, like lambs into the midst of
wolves, to share God's peace with the world. As sheep
in Christ's flock, let us share signs of peace with one another, that we too may have the courage to go forth, like
lambs into the midst of wolves, to share God's peace
with the world.

Response to the Word (Galatians 6, Luke 10)
Do you feel up to God's calling? Don't despair. God does
not call those who are equipped, God equips those who
are called. God has equipped you for the tasks ahead.
With gentleness and words of peace, let us look to the
welfare of our sisters and brothers in all that we say and
in all that we do.

Thanksgiving and Communion

Invitation to the Offering (Psalm 30)
Weeping may last the night, but joy comes with the
morning. God has turned our tears into shouts of
thanksgiving. Let us be grateful for the many blessings
in our lives, as we collect today's offering.

Offering Prayer (Galatians 6, Luke 10)
Bountiful God,
    the harvest is plentiful,
        but the laborers are few.
Through today's offerings,
    we pledge to be your laborers,
        that all may know the bounty of your harvest,
            and the gentleness of your peace. Amen.

Sending Forth

Benediction (Galatians 6, Luke 10)
Blessed by God to be a blessing to others:
Bear one another's burdens.
Correct one another with gentleness.
Heal one another with signs of peace.
If you do not grow weary in doing what is right,
you will reap a harvest of joy, hope and love.
Go with the peace of God.

July 10, 2016

Eighth Study after Pentecost, Proper 10
Karin Ellis

Color

Green

Scripture Readings

Amos 7:7-17; Psalm 82; Colossians 1:1-14; Luke 10:25-37

Theme Ideas

Today's scriptures depict God's mercy and justice, and how we live our lives according to God's ways. Amos, a poor herdsman, delivers the message that Israel will soon be in exile and the king will be dead. God has measured and weighed what the people have done, and they have come up short. The people will not be destroyed, but they will be relocated for a while. The psalmist proclaims the message of taking care of the weak and needy. Colossians provides a message of hope, as we see what life looks like when lived in the mercy and love of God. When our lives please God, we share the fruits of our labors and the fruits of our faith in Christ. Finally, Jesus tells the story of how mercy and hope were shared with a man who was beaten and left by the side of the road to die. A most unlikely stranger came to his aid, showed him mercy, and paid to nurse him back to life. These scriptures invite us to ask: How do we share God's mercy and love in the everyday moments of our lives?

Invitation and Gathering

Contemporary Gathering Words (Colossians 1, Luke 10)
Friends, come and learn how to bear good fruit
as you grow in the knowledge of God.
We are here to learn how to love God
with all our heart, soul, mind and strength.
—Or—

Contemporary Gathering Words (Colossians 1, Luke 10)
Our neighbor lies beaten in the ditch. Do we pass by, praising God in our hearts for the blessings in our lives, or do we see that God too is lying in the ditch and stop to help? Can we love God with all our heart, soul, mind, and not stop to help?
(B. J. Beu)

Call to Worship (Amos 7, Colossians 1, Luke 10)
From our busy lives, God calls us together
to worship and to pray.
    We are here, Holy One!
From different places, Christ calls us to gather,
to love, and to live.
    We are here, blessed Jesus!
From unexpected journeys, the Spirit calls us into unity
to serve and to grow.
    We are here, Holy Spirit!
Come! Let us worship.

Opening Prayer (Colossians 1, Luke 10)
Loving God, from the very beginning
    you have journeyed with your people.
Journey with us, this day,
    as we learn what it means to follow you.
Open our ears to your holy word.
Open our hearts to your love and compassion.
Open our hands to receive your grace
    and to share it with others.
Enable us to faithfully claim the name, "Christian,"
    as we strive to follow the ways and teachings
        of Jesus, the Christ.
Empower us with your Holy Spirit,
    as we worship you and serve one another.
In your holy name, we pray. Amen.

Proclamation and Response

Prayer of Confession (Amos 7, Colossians 1)
Gracious God, you offer us love and mercy,
    grace and forgiveness,
        yet we often turn away from you.
We live our lives according to what we want,
    not according to what you want for us.
We forget to care for one another.
We neglect your invitation to join you
    in an intimate relationship.
We fail to place you at the center of our lives.
We do not live our lives in response to your love
    and your grace.
Forgive us, O God.

Help us put you first in all that we do,
　　that we may dwell in your mercy and love,
　　　all the days of our lives. Amen.

Words of Assurance (Colossians 1, Luke 10)
　　Brothers and sisters, we are offered forgiveness
　　　and mercy through Christ.
　　Accept this gift and go forth bearing fruit for God!

Passing the Peace of Christ (Luke 10)
　　Who is our neighbor?
　　　Jesus tells us that everyone is our neighbor.
　　Let us greet our neighbor today as we share
　　　the peace of Christ!

Introduction to the Word
　　Gracious God, may we receive your holy word
　　　with open and loving hearts,
　　　　that our lives, and the lives around us,
　　　　　may be transformed. Amen.

Response to the Word (Colossians 1, Luke 10)
　　God of new life, thank you for what we have heard.
　　Thank you for the chance to hear the stories of our faith
　　　and ponder how these stories weave into our own.
　　May the words we have heard turn into actions
　　　of love, justice, and mercy. Amen.

Thanksgiving and Communion

Invitation to the Offering (Amos 7, Colossians 1)
　　To place God at the center of our lives, let us offer a portion of our gifts back to God, as we bring forth the fruits of our labor.

Offering Prayer (Luke 10)
>God of mercy, we bring these gifts to you
>>in thankfulness for all that you have done for us.
>May our gratitude turn into acts of mercy and justice,
>>and may these gifts help our neighbors
>>>both near and far. Amen.

Sending Forth

Benediction (Amos 7, Luke 10)
>Brothers and sisters, as we leave this place,
>>may our lives be centered on God,
>>and may our actions be examples
>>of Christ's love and mercy.
>Go in peace. Amen.

July 17, 2016

Ninth Sunday after Pentecost, Proper 11
B. J. Beu
[Copyright © 2015 by B. J. Beu. Used by permission.]

Color

Green

Scripture Readings

Amos 8:1-12; Psalm 52; Colossians 1:15-28;
Luke 10:38-42

Theme Ideas

Where judgment and lamentation pervade our Hebrew
Scriptures today, hope and assurance emerge in our
New Testament texts. Due to people's evil deeds, Amos
proclaims that God will bring a famine of the word—
they will seek it but find it not. And while the psalmist
warns of the impending destruction of those who do
evil, there is good news for the righteous—they will be
like green olive trees in the house of God. In Colossians,
Paul proclaims the good news that we are reconciled to
God in Christ. In Luke, Jesus reproofs Martha for being
distracted by her duties, even as he lifts up Mary, for
choosing the better part of sitting in his presence.

Invitation and Gathering

Contemporary Gathering Words (Psalm 52)
>The ungodly laugh in their conceit, plotting the destruction of the righteous with sharp tongues and works of treachery. They are fools. For the righteous are like green olive trees in the house of the Lord, and will dwell in God's steadfast love forever and ever.

Call to Worship (Psalm 52)
>Like green olive trees in the house of God,
>>**we come into God's presence.**
>
>Like young saplings in the courtyard of the Lord,
>>**we drink deep from the waters of life.**
>
>Like the fruit of God's vineyard,
>>**we ripen in the light of God.**
>
>Come, let us worship the Lord.

Opening Prayer (Amos 8, Psalm 52, Luke 10)
>Loving God,
>>your gift of abundant life
>>>is like a basket of summer fruit—
>>>>a delight to the eye
>>>>>and a pleasure to the tongue;
>>
>>your presence in our lives
>>>is like a green olive tree—
>>>>a joy to the heart
>>>>>and a blessing to the spirit.
>
>Speak to us your words of life,
>>that we may sit at your feet
>>>and know that we are yours. Amen.

Proclamation and Response

Prayer of Confession (Amos 8, Psalm 52, Colossians 1)
>Merciful God, buffeted by the winds of life,
>>we have grown weary
>>>and yearn for your hand to hold us.
>Pour forth your words of peace,
>>and bring us back to life.
>Forgive us when we are heedless
>>to the needs of others.
>Correct our ways when we are self-centered
>>and neglect the poor and powerless.
>Be our vision when we seek refuge
>>in our wealth and possessions.
>Draw us to you, Holy One,
>>and lead us into life. Amen.

Words of Assurance (Colossians 1)
>Hear the good news:
>>In Christ, we are united and reconciled with God
>Rejoice in the knowledge that we receive forgiveness
>>and abundant life in his name.

Passing the Peace of Christ (Colossians 1)
>Peace is a gift beyond price. In Christ, we find peace as we are reconciled to God. Let us share this precious gift with one another in joy and thanksgiving.

Invitation to the Word (Amos 8)
>Our hearts are famished.
>>**We are hungry for God's word.**
>From sea to sea, we listen but do not hear.
>>**From north to south, and east to west,**
>>**we seek God's word, but find it not.**

Our hearts are famished.
We are hungry for God's word.

Response to the Word (Luke 10)
Loving Teacher,
you ask us to sit with you
and care for our souls.
Your presence is more to be desired
than bread and honey,
more to be sought than course meats
and fine wine.
Bless our understanding of the lessons
you would teach us. Amen.
—Or—

Response to the Word
This is the word of God for the people of God.
Thanks be to God.

Thanksgiving and Communion

Offering Prayer (Amos 8)
Loving God,
you fill our lives to overflowing
like baskets of summer fruit.
May the offering we return to you this day
show our gratitude for your many blessings,
and our commitment to love our neighbors
as you have loved us.
Through your goodness
and the sharing of these gifts,
may all come to know
the richness of your love. Amen.

Sending Forth

Benediction (Psalm 52)

Though we may leave God's house,
we do not leave God's presence.
Like green olive trees in the house of God,
our roots go deep in the soil of holy love.
Know that God's presence goes with us
as we go forth to share God's love for all.

July 24, 2016

Tenth Study after Pentecost, Proper 12
Laura Jaquith Bartlett

Color

Green

Scripture Readings

Hosea 1:2-10; Psalm 85; Colossians 2:6-15 (16-19);
Luke 11:1-13

Theme Ideas

What does it look like when truth springs up from the
ground and righteousness gazes down from heaven? I live
in a forest, so my mind immediately pictures giant ma-
ple leaves floating down from the sky...daffodil shoots
pushing up through last year's leaves...wildly shaped
mushrooms sprouting out of decaying logs...shafts of
sunlight streaming through the dense trees. These visions
are glimpses of God's grace: anger turning into faithful
love; hurt and rejection transforming into faith and forgiveness; fear and despair dissolving into the warm embrace of God's limitless love—a love that is all-forgiving,
all-encompassing, all-embracing.

Invitation and Gathering

Contemporary Gathering Words (Hosea 1, Psalm 85, Luke 11)

> Come in, angry people!
> **This is a safe place to vent your fury.**
> Come in, hurting ones!
> **Here you will find compassion and grace**
> **to heal your wounds.**
> Come in, all who are in need of love and peace.
> **Here, we gather as children of the living God.**

Call to Worship (Psalm 85)

> Lord, you've been kind to your land.
> **You've changed our circumstances for the better!**
> You are the God who saves us.
> **You've forgiven your people's wrongdoing.**
> Because of you, O God, faithful love and truth have met.
> **Righteousness and peace have kissed.**

Opening Prayer (Hosea 1, Psalm 85, Luke 11)

> Here we are, God,
>   your children.
> We go astray,
>   yet you forgive us.
> We get angry at others,
>   but you keep loving us.
> We ask you for a thousand different things,
>   and you respond by showering us with blessings.
> You offer us salvation, mercy, and love.
> Thank you, God, for inviting us
>   into this grace-filled relationship.

We pray in the name of the one
    who showed us what grace looks like,
        Jesus Christ. Amen.

Proclamation and Response

Prayer of Confession and Words of Assurance (Hosea 1, Psalm 85, Luke 11)

Dear God, you have every right to be angry with us.
We have such good intentions,
    but we continue to mess up.
    Forgive us, God.
We joyfully sing of your love on Sunday morning,
    but by Monday, we're feeling lost and unlovable.
    Forgive us, God.
We preach tolerance and compassion,
    but we find ourselves raging at the guy
        who cuts us off in traffic.
    Forgive us, God.
(Silence)
Then you forgive our sins,
    and once more show us how to forgive others.
You offer us a vision of truth and love meeting together,
    and you invite us into their warm embrace.
    Thank you, God.
As your forgiven people,
    beloved children of your promise,
        you renew us in holy love.
    Thank you, God. Amen.

Passing the Peace of Christ (Psalm 85)

Psalm 85 paints a beautiful picture of righteousness and peace kissing each other. Imagine right now what that might look like *(pause)*. Remember, this is the same psalm that also speaks of God's burning anger! Some of you may be harboring anger toward another—or at least some minor irritation or frustration. As you rise to offer one another signs of Christ's peace, picture God's faithful love and truth meeting together in an embrace.

Response to the Word (Hosea 1, Psalm 85, Luke 11)

(This response is designed to be read by two persons in quick succession. There should be no spoken introduction or conclusion; allow the "script" to speak for itself.)

Annoyed
> *Irritated*

Angry
> *Offended*

Furious
> *Seething*

Raging
> *Incensed*

Livid
> *Irate*

How could you do this to me?
(Pause, as both readers look at each other)

Hurt
> *Dejected*

Rejected
> *Stupid*

Regretful
> *Sorry*

Ashamed
> *Contrite*

Lonely
> *Forlorn*

Please forgive me!
(Pause, as both readers look at each other)

Mercy
> Hope

Grace
> Forgiveness

Salvation
> Pardon

Compassion
> Faithfulness

Truth
> Love

Love
> Love

God!
(Readers embrace each other)

Thanksgiving and Communion

Offering Prayer (Luke 11)

Generous God, just as your Son taught us how to pray,
> he also taught us how to share with those in need.

When a neighbor knocks at our door needing bread,
> we know how to respond.

When people in our community are hungry,
> we know how to respond.

When sisters and brothers around the world are hurting,
> we know how to respond.

Thank you for this opportunity
> to turn prayer into action.

Amen.

Sending Forth

Benediction (Hosea 1, Psalm 85, Luke 11)
Go in peace,
knowing that you are forgiven people.
Go in faith,
knowing that God hears your prayers
and understands your needs.
Go in love,
knowing that God invites you
into the holy embrace
of truth
and righteousness.
Go now as children of the living God
to serve others in Christ's name. Amen.

July 31, 2016

Eleventh Study after Pentecost, Proper 13
Susan A. Blain

Color

Green

Scripture Readings

Hosea 11:1-11; Psalm 107:1-9, 43; Colossians 3:1-11;
Luke 12:13-21

Theme Ideas

Hosea 11 offers a rare glimpse in scripture of a tender,
parenting God. And while there is some ambiguity as to
whether this is an image of God as Father or as Mother, we may choose to lift up the motherly qualities of a
Holy One intimately involved with the young and fragile people Israel.

Invitation and Gathering

Contemporary Gathering Words (Hosea 11:9b)
I am God and no mortal, the Holy One in your midst,
and I will not come in wrath.

Call to Worship (Hosea 11)

Reach out with uncertain hands.

Our steadfast Mother will teach us to walk!

Raise your hungry voices.

Our generous Mother will feed us!

Cry out when you are lost.

Our yearning Mother will call us home.

Let us rejoice and worship this Holy, Tender One.

Opening Prayer (Psalm 107, Colossians 3)

Beckoning God, you call your people
    from the north and the south,
        the east and the west.
You long to gather us,
    from the places we have wandered,
        into a community of love and justice.
End our wanderings here today.
Open our eyes,
    that we may recognize your presence among us,
        and clothe ourselves in your mercy and grace.
In Jesus' name, we pray. Amen.

Proclamation and Response

Prayer of Confession (Colossians 3)

So many forces work to tear apart the fragile fabric of a faith community: Promiscuity, greed (as bad as idolatry!), malice, slander, abusive language, lies. The list goes on and on! Let us take a moment in silent prayer to reflect upon the behaviors we need to overcome—where our actions tear down instead of build up our common life; where our actions dishonor the presence of the Holy One in our midst, who creates us in the

Divine image, and calls us into beloved community.
(Silence prayer follows)

Words of Assurance (Colossians 3:10)
Hear the good news:
In Christ we have been raised from death to life;
we have been forgiven and made whole,
and clothed with new life in the image of God.

Passing the Peace of Christ (Colossians 3)
Let us greet our sisters and brothers, who bear the image of the beauty of God, by passing the peace of Christ.

Introduction to the Word (Psalm 107)
O give thanks to our God, who is so good.
God's steadfast love endures forever!

Response to the Word (Psalm 107)
Let those who are wise pay attention to these things, and consider the steadfast love of God!

Thanksgiving and Communion

Invitation to the Offering (Luke 12:21)
Today's Gospel story calls us to "be rich toward God"—to share generously, in this moment, with our community and our world. Let us give abundantly of what we have been given, that we may meet the needs of neighbors near and far.

Offering Prayer
Holy One in our midst,
take our offerings and bless them,

that they may multiply and be a blessing
in your world.
In Jesus' name, we pray. Amen.

Sending Forth

Benediction (Hosea 11, Colossians 3, Luke 12)
May our good God mother us to maturity,
    clothe us in her image, and empower us
    to live with love and generosity in our world.

August 7, 2016

Twelfth Sunday after Pentecost, Proper 14
Mary J. Scifres

Color

Green

Scripture Readings

Isaiah 1:1, 10-20; Psalm 50:1-8, 22-23;
Hebrews 11:1-3, 8-16; Luke 12:32-40

Theme Ideas

True treasure comes when we share with others, when we care for others, and when we love others as God has loved us. This is the treasure God seeks from us. This is the treasure we are called to accumulate during our time on earth. When we lose sight of this treasure, we fail to follow the lineage of faith. But when we keep our eyes on the prize of mercy and justice, we become treasures to God. Isaiah laments when the Israelites offer empty worship, and calls them to cleanse themselves by learning "to do good" (v. 17). Jesus comforts and encourages us when he calls us to be like bridesmaids with well-stocked lamps, awaiting the bridegroom.

These reminders of the mutual partnership we share with God, as we create Christ's realm on earth, are calls to bring true treasure to our lives and to God's world.

Invitation and Gathering

Contemporary Gathering Words (Luke 12)
Don't be afraid of God. Come with the confidence of children and beloved partners, for God delights in giving us abundant life and steadfast love.

Call to Worship (Psalm 50, Luke 12)
From the rising of the sun…
God speaks, calling out to the earth.
At the beginning of each new day…
God speaks, calling us to life and service.
Even with the setting sun…
God speaks, reminding us that we are not alone.
As we gather for worship this day
**God speaks, inviting us to love freely
and to become true treasure on earth.**

Opening Prayer (Isaiah 1, Luke 12)
Mighty God, speak your truth to us this day.
Give us the treasure of your wisdom and love,
that we might become for the world
the treasure you seek us to be.
Clothe us with your compassion and courage,
that we might be Christ to a hurting world.
In your holy name, we pray. Amen.

Proclamation and Response

Prayer of Confession (Isaiah 1)
Wash us with your grace, O God,
and cleanse us with your forgiveness.
Remove from us
the evil we harbor in our hearts.
Transform our deeds of shame
into acts of righteousness,
that we might learn your goodness
and be instruments of your mercy.
In your holy name, we pray. Amen.

Words of Assurance (Luke 12)
Don't be afraid, little flock,
for God delights in giving us the kingdom,
the treasure of God's mercy and love!
With delight and grace, we are forgiven
and loved by God!

Passing the Peace of Christ (Luke 12)
Let us share the treasure of love and mercy with one
another as we offer the peace of Christ.

Introduction to the Word (Isaiah 1)
Hear God's word.
Listen to God's teaching,
for this holy word is a gift to be treasured and lived.

Response to the Word (Isaiah 1, Luke 12)
God calls us to lives of goodness and mercy.
We are ready to seek justice
and to help the oppressed.

God calls us to be dressed for service.
We are ready to protect the weak
and to shelter those in need.
God calls us to build treasures of love.
We are ready to show compassion
and to offer kindness to those we meet.
God calls us to have lamps ready to light the way.
We are ready to shine Christ's light
and to illuminate the world with love!
(This litany leads effectively into Strathdee's "I Am the Light
of the World," "Keep Your Lamps Trimmed and Burning" or
Curtis Mayfield's "People, Get Ready.")

Thanksgiving and Communion

Invitation to the Offering (Luke 12)
In this time of offering, bring the treasure of your love.
Share gifts that will bring love to God's world. Through
the sharing of our gifts for our church's mission and
ministry, we are building Christ's realm here on earth.

Offering Prayer (Luke 12)
As we offer these earthly treasures back to you,
transform these gifts into love and mercy
by the power of your Holy Spirit
and the gift of your miraculous love.
Turn these earthly treasures of human currency
into heavenly treasures of love and justice
to bring your realm here on earth.

Great Thanksgiving (Isaiah 1, Luke 4:18-19)
We give you thanks, our creator and liberator,
for by your Word you have called forth creation,

and created us in your image.
You led us from slavery to freedom,
    going before us with cloud and fiery pillar.
With burning coals you gave utterance to the prophets,
    to demand that justice roll down like waters,
    and righteousness like an ever-flowing stream.
In the fullness of time, your Spirit descended
    like a dove upon Jesus, anointing him:
    to preach good news to the poor,
    to proclaim release to the captives,
    to offer recovery of sight to the blind,
    to set at liberty those who were oppressed,
    and to declare the reign of God in our midst.
When Jesus gathered with the ones he loved,
    he was known to them in the breaking of bread.
Before feeding the multitudes,
    he broke bread and gave thanks.
When two or three were gathered together,
    he broke bread and gave thanks.
He sought the outcasts and broke bread with them,
    witnessing the fullness of your grace.
On the night of his greatest trial,
    he gathered his friends together in an upper room
    and said to them:
"Tonight, I am going to create
    a sustaining community among you.
It will not require you to always be faithful,
    or perfect, or good, or right, or powerful,
    or unblemished, or pure.
It will not require you to hold an advanced degree
    or to have the proper wealth, skin color,
    sexual identity, gender or religion.

This community, we are creating tonight,
    requires two things:
    your willingness to share with one another,
    and your remembrance of me.
These two are enough to bind you to one another,
    and to your work on behalf of the world."
Jesus said: "Take this bread, the bread of life:
    It represents my physical presence,
    which has been with you on many adventures,
    and the bodies of all who have tried to love mercy,
    create justice, and build the kingdom of God
    here on earth.
Whenever you eat bread, remember this evening.
Think on what we have tried to do for the poor
    and those who are marginalized.
Take this cup, the cup of salvation:
    It represents the covenant we make
    with one another to always be there for one another;
It also represents my promise to be with you always.
This cup and your thoughts of me will sustain you
    and restore your spirits."
(Joanne Brown)

Giving the Bread and Cup

(The bread and wine are given to the people, with these or other words of blessing.)
Take and eat. May your hunger for justice
    strengthen you to bring God's realm here on earth.
Take and drink. May your thirst for mercy
    lead you to streams of abundant love
    for a world in need of justice and hope.

Sending Forth

Benediction (Luke 12)
People, get ready!
We are dressed for service.
People, get ready!
The world needs our love.
People, get ready!
We go forth to shine Christ's light in the world!

August 14, 2016

Thirteenth Sunday after Pentecost, Proper 15
Deborah Sokolove

Color

Green

Scripture Readings

Isaiah 5:1-7; Psalm 80:1-2, 8-19; Hebrews 11:29–12:2; Luke 12:49-56

Theme Ideas

Those who have gone before us show us what it means to live lives of faith by following Jesus no matter what the obstacles may be. God wants us, also, to be faithful witnesses to the power of Christ in our lives, that we too may bring God's justice into the brokenness of our world.

Invitation and Gathering

Contemporary Gathering Words (Psalm 80, Hebrews 11–12)
We are surrounded by a great cloud of witnesses. Strengthen us, Holy One. Let your face shine upon us, and keep us safe.

Call to Worship (Psalm 80, Hebrews 11–12, Luke 12)
By faith, God's people passed through the Red Sea.
By faith, the walls of Jericho fell.
**We come in faith, calling on the name of God
to save us.**
Is a cloud rising in the west?
Is the south wind blowing?
**We come in faith, calling on the name of God
to save us.**
We are surrounded by a great cloud of witnesses,
who show us the way to run the race set before us.
**Strengthen us, Holy One.
Let your face shine upon us and keep us safe.**

Opening Prayer (Isaiah 5, Psalm 80, Hebrews 11–12)
Shepherd of Israel, God of hosts, Spirit of faith,
you lead us like a beacon
on a dark and difficult road.
Like a gardener, you have planted us and cared for us—
nurturing the soil of our lives,
and pruning our branches,
that we might bring forth
tender new shoots.
You give us life and call us to bear good fruit—
to administer justice,
to quench the fires of hatred,
and to live in love and service of the world.
Help us run the race you have set before us,
that we might join that great cloud of witnesses
whose faith gave them the strength
to show the world what it means
to follow Jesus. Amen.

Proclamation and Response

Prayer of Confession (Isaiah 5)
> Shepherd of Israel, God of hosts, Spirit of faith,
>> you have planted us like choice vines,
>>> expecting us to yield sweet grapes,
>>>> good fruit with which to feed the world.
>> **Yet, we have yielded wild grapes,**
>>> **bitter fruit unfit for eating.**
> You have cleared the way for us,
>> digging the earth and removing stones,
>>> expecting us to bear the sweet fruit
>>>> of justice and righteousness
>>>>> for a hungry and hurting world.
>> **Yet, the fruit we yield is bitter,**
>>> **as bloodshed and evil are done in our name.**
> Forgive us, Holy One,
>> for ignoring the cries of anguish
>>> that rise up to you.
>> **Restore us, God of hosts,**
>>> **that we might yield good fruit**
>>>> **to feed a hungry world. Amen.**

Words of Assurance (Psalm 80, Hebrews 11–12)
> God fills us with life and love,
>> offering us forgiveness and grace
>>> whenever we call on the name of the Holy One.
> In the name of Christ, you are forgiven.
>> **In the name of Christ, you are forgiven.**
>> **Thanks be to God. Amen.**

Passing the Peace of Christ (Hebrews 11–12)
> As forgiven and beloved people of God, let us offer one
> another signs of peace.

The peace of Christ be with you.
The peace of Christ be with you always.

Response to the Word (Luke 12)
Holy One, you invite us into a baptism of fire,
warning us that your word often brings strife.
Give us the faith of that great cloud of witnesses
who went before us, that we too
might interpret the signs in our own day.

Thanksgiving and Communion

Offering Prayer (Isaiah 5, Hebrews 11–12)
Shepherd of Israel, God of hosts, Spirit of faith,
you went to the cross with joy for our sake.
We offer ourselves as a living sacrifice,
bringing the fruits of our labors
to the foot of the cross.

Great Thanksgiving
Christ be with you.
And also with you.
Lift up your hearts.
We lift them up to God.
Let us give our thanks to the Holy One.
It is right to give our thanks and praise.

It is a right, good, and a joyful thing,
always and everywhere, to give our thanks to you,
who brought the people through the Red Sea
as if it were dry land,
brought down the walls of Jericho,
and saved Rahab to be a foremother of Jesus.

You clear the ground for the vine that is your people,
  allowing us to take deep root and fill the earth,
  bringing us to fruitful life.
And so, with your creatures on earth
  and all the heavenly chorus, we praise your name
  and join their unending hymn:
  Holy, holy, holy Lord, God of power and might,
    heaven and earth are full of your glory.
  Hosanna in the highest. Blessed is the one
    who comes in the name of the Lord.
  Hosanna in the highest.
Holy are you, and holy is your child, Jesus Christ,
  who warns us of dangers to come,
  and bids us to be aware of the signs of the times.
On the night in which he gave himself up,
  Jesus took bread, gave thanks to you,
  broke the bread, and gave it to the disciples, saying:
  "Take, eat; this is my body which is given for you.
  Do this in remembrance of me."
When the supper was over, Jesus took the cup,
  offered thanks and gave it to the disciples, saying:
  "Drink from this, all of you;
  this is my life in the new covenant,
  poured out for you and for many,
  for the forgiveness of sins.
  Do this, as often as you drink it,
  in remembrance of me."
And so, in remembrance of your mighty acts
  in Jesus Christ, we proclaim the mystery of faith.
  Christ has died.
  Christ is risen.
  Christ will come again.

Pour out your Holy Spirit on our gathering,
and on these gifts of bread and wine.
Make them be for us the body and blood of Christ,
that we may be the body of Christ
to a world that longs for peace.

Shepherd of Israel, God of hosts, Spirit of faith,
we give our thanks and praise to you.
Amen.

Sending Forth

Benediction (Hebrews 11–12)
Like the martyrs who suffered and died,
witnessing to the power of Christ in their lives,
let our lives be a witness to the power of Christ
in our lives, as we go out in faithful service
to the world.
And may the grace of Christ, the love of God,
and the life of the Spirit be with you,
and in you, and around you. Amen.

August 21, 2016

Fourteenth Sunday after Pentecost, Proper 16
Bill Hoppe

Color

Green

Scripture Readings

Jeremiah 1:4-10; Psalm 71:1-6, 13-18; Hebrews 12:18-29;
Luke 13:10-17

Theme Ideas

We are called and created to embody the word of God.
So innate is this purpose, according to the prophet Jeremiah and the psalmist, that it becomes an inseparable
part of our very being, even before we are born. How
can we refuse the voice of the One who forms us, who
shields and saves us, who heals and perfects us, and
who completes us in love? All that we were, all that we
are, and all that we will be... all this proclaims the living
Word.

Invitation and Gathering

Contemporary Gathering Words (Jeremiah 1, Psalm 71, Hebrews 12, Luke 13)

The irresistible word of God calls to us and through us. A fortress and refuge built upon a rock, God's word is at once terrifying, awesome, revered, and holy. God's word lives and breathes—it cannot be confined to printed characters upon a page. God speaks and we are created. Jesus, the living Word, cries out and we are healed.

Call to Worship (Psalm 71, Hebrews 12)

We stand before the city of the living God.
Hear the song of God's children!
Hear the voice of the One who speaks from heaven!
The voice of the Lord shakes the earth
and echoes through the cosmos!
God's kingdom is unshakable,
a rock that cannot be moved.
The Lord is our refuge.
God's kingdom stands forever!
Give thanks to the Lord!
We worship together to praise our God!

Opening Prayer (Jeremiah 1, Hebrews 12)

Living Word, whose voice holds us spellbound,
we gather to hear what you would say
to us this day.
Let your precepts fill our ears
and open our mouths to speak your truth.
Let your teachings pervade our very lives—
to uproot and to pull down,

to change and to renew,
    to build and to plant.
In your presence, we gather to worship
    in reverence and in awe. Amen.

Proclamation and Response

Prayer of Confession (Jeremiah 1, Psalm 71, Luke 13)
    Lord, you are my beginning and my ending.
    Before I was born,
        even before I was formed in my mother's womb,
            I am with you.
    Even when I die and travel onward,
        I am with you.
    You are my hope.
    In you I place my trust.
    In times of weakness when my spirit fails,
        you are the rock to which I cling.
    In times of struggle when I am bent with affliction,
        you heal me.
    In times of shame when my eyes are downcast,
        you forgive me and raise me up.
    I will lean upon you all the days of my life.
    You are my praise, forever and ever. Amen.

Words of Assurance (Psalm 71, Luke 13)
    There are those who will tell us what can't be done,
        what shouldn't be done, what mustn't be done.
    And then there is God, who says what should be done,
        what must be done, what will be done!
    When we listen to God and follow God's ways,
        we are forgiven and saved.
    Those who have ears, let them hear.

Passing the Peace of Christ (Jeremiah 1, Luke 13)
Speak and share healing words of peace with one another, just as Jesus spoke to the crippled woman at the
synagogue and set her free to praise God. Have no fear
of what you should say. Simply speak from the heart
and God's voice will be heard.

Response to the Word (Jeremiah 1, Hebrews 12, Luke 13)
Your voice is indescribable, Lord.
It consumes us like a fire.
It commands our attention like a fanfare.
It unlocks the shackles that fetter your Spirit
    and innovation.
Fill us with your renewing word,
    and create us anew. Amen.

Thanksgiving and Communion

Invitation to the Offering (Jeremiah 1, Psalm 71, Hebrews 12, Luke 13)
Teacher, you have taught us all that we know.
Savior, you have delivered us from death.
Guide, you have given us purpose.
Healer, you have made us whole.
Lord, you have given us all that we need.
In gratitude and thanks,
    may we offer our gifts back to you
    as we collect today's offering.

Offering Prayer (Hebrews 12, Luke 13)
Holy One, you have shared with us
    the riches of your kingdom—
    treasures unlike anything

we have ever seen with our eyes
     or touched with our hands.
We rejoice in all the wonderful things
     you have done for us and given to us!
Receive these offerings this day,
     as we worship you in the name of Jesus. Amen.

Sending Forth

Benediction (Jeremiah 1, Psalm 71)
     Go where God sends you.
     Speak what the Lord has given you to say.
     Have no fear, God is with you.
     God is your hope and your praise!

August 28, 2016

Fifteenth Sunday after Pentecost, Proper 17
Safiyah Fosua

Color

Green

Scripture Readings

Jeremiah 2:4-13; Psalm 81:1,10-16,
Hebrews 13:1-8, 15-16; Luke 14:1, 7-14

Theme Ideas

There is a moment of serendipity between the humility of Luke 14:7-14 and the hospitality of Hebrews 13.
It could very well be that humility and hospitality
are first cousins, or at least close friends, because it
takes a good measure of humility to offer the kind of
hospitality that puts the comfort and needs of one's
guest ahead of our own—particularly when that guest
is a stranger. And, it takes a certain measure of humility to resist the temptation to be the star at another person's dinner party, as Jesus advises in today's parable
from Luke.

Invitation and Gathering

Contemporary Gathering Words (Hebrews 13)

What if?
What if the stranger in the pews
Is really
Somebody
Test driving our church
To see how *we* are?

What if
God really *did* appear in a dream to
The couple in the back
Telling them that you and your church
Could be trusted
To care
That their squalling infant
Is actually sick unto death
And her young parents
Are about to fall apart?

What if
The teen in the hoodie
Is here
Because *he* does not approve
Of the substances
Snorted, injected, or consumed
By the adults in his household?
Here,
Because he is
Determined
To turn away from destruction
By turning to God?

What if
We really do
Entertain *angels*
Unawares?

Call to Worship (Hebrews 13, Luke 14)
You have come to a community of love and hospitality.
Here, God entreats us to see strangers
as angels in disguise.
You have come to a community of worship.
Here, praising God is more important
than puffing ourselves up.
Here, you are God's honored guest.

Opening Prayer
Here we are before you, God,
either poor in pocket or poor in spirit—
confidently, unashamedly here,
because you invited us.
Here we are, God,
knowing firsthand what it is like
to be maimed and handicapped by life,
yet welcomed into your presence.
Here we are again, God,
like John Newton, once blind
but now able to see.
For your invitation to be part of your family
and part of this family,
we thank you.
May we be eager to extend the same welcome,
and the same hospitality,
to others in your name. Amen.

Proclamation and Response

Prayer of Confession (Luke 14)

God, we come to you today
  confessing our love of the first chair.
The seeds of "healthy competition" sown in childhood
  have borne misshapen fruit in adulthood.
We love the best seats, bask in recognition,
  and covet the "edge" that brings us honor.
Forgive us, God, when our competitiveness
  yields more pride than excellence.
Forgive us, God, when we forget that we work for you,
  and not for ourselves.
Forgive us, God, when we forget that humility
  and hospitality are close relatives,
    and that those who would be your disciples
      are called to hold hands with the stranger.
Make us less eager to fight for power and position
  and more willing to make room for those
    who have neither name nor strength. Amen.

Words of Assurance (Luke 14, Hebrews 13)

Those who exalt themselves will be humbled,
  but those who humble themselves will be exalted.
In faith, you have made your humble confession
  before the living God who continues to offer us
  forgiveness through Jesus Christ,
    who is the same yesterday, today, and forever.
In the name of Jesus Christ, you are forgiven. Amen.

Response to the Word (James 4, Luke 14)

Whom does God exalt?
  God resists and opposes the proud,
  but gives grace to those who are humble.

Whom does Jesus exalt?
**Those who exalt themselves will be humbled,
but those who humble themselves will be exalted!**
Whom does the Spirit exalt?
Those who exalt God!

Thanksgiving and Communion

Offering Prayer (Hebrews 13)
God, here we are,
offering in hand,
standing with faith
that what we offer to you
matters to the work of the kingdom.
God, here we are,
remembering the pennies and nickels and dimes
of grandmothers and widows
that built many of our buildings
struggling not to compare their rich faith
to ours.
Most Holy God,
we ask that you use these gifts
to increase your kingdom,
and to increase our faith in your work. Amen.

Sending Forth

Benediction
Go from this place, remembering that God thinks highly
of the lowly and the stranger.
**Today we leave with a renewed commitment
to take the lowest seat, to be content
with what we have, and be kind to those
who can never repay us. Amen.**

September 4, 2016

Sixteenth Sunday after Pentecost, Proper 18
Rebecca Gaudino

Color

Green

Scripture Readings

Jeremiah 18:1-11; Psalm 139:1-6, 13-18; Philemon 1-21;
Luke 14:25-33

Theme Ideas

Spoken to a Greco-Roman world thoroughly divided by
understandings of social status, today's New Testament
texts present an amazing vision of the family of Christ.
Kinship and a system of patronage determined possi-
bility in the ancient world. In Luke, Jesus presents two
radical principles that energize his new family. First,
this family is not determined by bloodline—it is founded in Jesus Christ. Second, being whole-heartedly, and
single-mindedly, committed to Christ's vision is what
fleshes out this new family. In Philemon, we read a case
study of this vision as it is put into practice. Choosing
his words with utmost care, Paul argues lovingly for a
new relationship between two men, owner and slave,

by referring to the slave as "my own heart" and "beloved brother" (Philemon vv. 12, 16; use the NSRV for
the familial language of the Greek.)

Invitation and Gathering

Contemporary Gathering Words (Philemon)

> One: Friends! Co-workers!
> *Women: Brothers!*
> Men: Sisters!
> Adults: Followers of Christ!
> Youth: Saints of the church!
> One: Welcome, one and all! Welcome home!
> *Women: This is the place to be refreshed and encouraged.*
> Men: This is the place of acceptance and love!
> One: Blessings of grace and peace to you all!
> **All: Amen! Amen! Amen!**

Call to Worship (Philemon)

> Grace to you, and peace from God our maker
> and from the Lord Jesus Christ!
> Welcome, friends and coworkers in Christ!
> Greetings, brothers and sisters!
> **We come to rejoice in the love**
> **and encouragement of our family in Christ.**
> **We come for the joyful reminder**
> **that God accepts and loves us.**

Opening Prayer (Philemon, Luke 14)

> God of love, we are your family,
> brothers and sisters all,
> sharing in your vision and work.

We give you thanks for the many ways
> you have loved and blessed us,
>> encouraged and renewed us.
We thank you for the times we have experienced joy,
> and for the knowledge that you love and accept us.
We bring our joy and gratitude to you today
> as we sing our thanksgiving and praise. Amen.

Proclamation and Response

Prayer of Confession (Philemon)

Jesus Christ, giver of love and peace,
> we are grateful for your vision of humankind—
>> a vision that embraces all,
>>> leaving none behind.
You call us your brothers and sisters,
> even when we do not recognize this truth.
Forgive us when we look down on others,
> failing to see them as our sisters and brothers.
Forgive us when kinship is not a priority in our lives.
Open our hearts to everyone in your family,
> that they may become our family, too.
In your name, brother of us all, we pray. Amen.

Words of Assurance (Philemon)

The blessings of grace and peace are ours,
> through God our maker,
>> and Jesus Christ our savior.
Forgiven and peace are ours. Amen!

Passing the Peace of Christ (Philemon)

Friends, co-workers, sisters, brothers, followers of Christ, saints of the Church, let us greet one another with the peace and love of our brother, the Lord Jesus Christ.

Response to the Word (Philemon, Luke 14)
To God, we lift our hearts.
**Praise be to God, our maker,
for the vision that inspires us!
Praise be to our Lord, Jesus Christ,
for the example that teaches us!
Praise be to the Holy Spirit, our comforter,
for the energy that brings us new life!**

Thanksgiving and Communion

Invitation to the Offering (Philemon 4)
The words Paul spoke long ago can be spoken here today: "I thank my God every time I mention you in my prayers because I've heard of your love both for the Lord Jesus and for all God's people." What this ancient church was doing long ago, we are doing today whenever we uphold the work of Jesus Christ in the world. Let us give joyfully to this work, out of the same spirit of love that Paul blessed in the ancient church.

Offering Prayer (Philemon)
Big-hearted God,
we thank you for accepting us as we are—
rich in some ways, poor in others.
You see us just as we are,
and you love us wholeheartedly.
Your generous love gives us confidence
to live our lives in a world
where it's hard to find acceptance.

We give the gift of our lives and resources to you,
    that others may experience this love,
        and find new confidence for living
            as children of your love.
    Bless these gifts, and multiply our family
        in Jesus Christ. Amen.

Sending Forth

Benediction (Philemon)
    Friends and coworkers, sisters and brothers,
    let's share our faith in a God of love and acceptance.
        Followers of Christ, saints of the church,
        let's open our hearts and our families
        to those who need to know God's love.
    May the grace and peace of God our maker,
    and the Lord Jesus Christ, bless us as we go.
        Amen.

September 11, 2016

Seventeenth Sunday after Pentecost, Proper 19
B. J. Beu

[Copyright © 2015 by B. J. Beu. Used by permission.]

Color

Green

Scripture Readings

Jeremiah 4:11-12, 22-28; Psalm 14:1-7; 1 Timothy 1:12-17; Luke 15:1-10

Theme Ideas

Today's scriptures epitomize why people can't make heads or tails of the Bible. Jeremiah prophesies utter desolation and misery as a consequence of human ignorance and sin. The psalmist, likewise, speaks of human faithlessness and depravity, and a world devoid of God's followers. But Paul writes of amazing grace and God's boundless mercy, and Jesus promises that heaven rejoices when sinners repent. So which is it? Does God plan to smite us, or does God yearn to bless us as we find our way? As a sweep through salvation history, these scriptures remind us that the journey of faith is one of failure and forgiveness—a journey involving

both judgment and mercy. Just plan to spend a little ex-
tra time on Sunday to sort things out.

Invitation and Gathering

Contemporary Gathering Words (Luke 15)
When we are lost and alone, when we are afraid and far
from home, do not despair. Turn to the One who seeks
the lost and rejoices in those who are found. Set aside
doubt and despair. It's time to return home.

Call to Worship (Psalm 14, 1 Timothy 1, Luke 15)
Fools and sages...
come to the throne of grace.
All are welcome here.
Those who are lost and hoping to be found...
come find a home at the seat of glory.
All are welcome here.
Sinners and saints...
come to the place of new beginnings.
All are welcome here.

Opening Prayer (Psalm 14, Luke 15)
God of heaven and earth,
though we often go astray,
we seek your love and mercy;
though we abide with fools
who say in their hearts,
"There is no God,"
our hearts belong to you.
Be our Shepherd, and guide our ways,
for we are weary of wandering lost and afraid,
and long to be welcomed home. Amen.

Proclamation and Response

Prayer of Confession (Jeremiah 4, Psalm 14, 1 Timothy 1, Luke 15)
>Hot winds blow through the deserts of our lives, O God.
>Our souls feel dry and parched.
>How long will your anger burn against us?
>Call us into the green pastures of your love once more,
>>and we will rejoice with the angels above.
>Guide us in the path of righteousness,
>>that we may forsake our foolish ways
>>>and be a friend to those
>>>>who seek to find their way.
>Reclaim us as your own,
>>and we will not forsake
>>>the knowledge you impart to us. Amen.

Words of Assurance (1 Timothy 1)
>With overflowing grace,
>>Christ Jesus came to save us.
>With steadfast love,
>>the King of kings leads us into eternal life.

Passing the Peace (Luke 15)
>Let us bring joy in heaven as we sweep out our spiritual houses and share the peace that only God can bring.

Response to the Word (Jeremiah 4, Psalm 14, Luke 15)
>When all seems lost in our lives,
>>restore our fortunes, O God.
>When the brokenness of life threatens to overcome us,
>>find us and heal us, Holy One.
>When the terrors of the night fill us with fear,
>>comfort us and lead us home. Amen.

Thanksgiving and Communion

Offering Prayer (Psalm 14)
> O great deliverer,
>> when we fall on hard times,
>>> you are there to restore our fortunes;
>> when we lack for food and nourishment,
>>> you feed us from your hand;
>> when we wander as a stranger,
>>> you make us family.
> Receive our thanks and gratitude,
>> as we share these gifts
>>> with a world in need. Amen.

Sending Forth

Benediction (1 Timothy 1, Luke 15)
> Welcomed here by God,
>> **God sends us forth to serve.**
> Called here by Christ,
>> **Christ sends us forth to love.**
> Made whole by the Spirit,
>> **the Spirit sends us forth to care.**

September 18, 2016

Eighteenth Sunday after Pentecost, Proper 20
Mary J. Scifres

[Copyright © 2015 by Mary J. Scifres. Used by permission.]

Color

Green

Scripture Readings

Jeremiah 8:18–9:1; Psalm 79:1-9; 1 Timothy 2:1-7;
Luke 16:1-13

Theme Ideas

Squandering property, embezzling from your boss,
worshiping idols, facing God's judgment...these are
the missteps that frame today's scriptures. Timothy calls
us to pray for our leaders: "so that we can lead a quiet
and peaceful life" (v. 2)—a reminder that leaders who
squander, embezzle or create false gods will bring strife
and sorrow to us all. Our world is not an easy place to
follow God. But even in this challenging world, Christ
is our mediator, answering our prayers when we cry
out: "God...help us.... / Deliver us and cover our sins"
(Psalm 79:9).

Invitation and Gathering

Contemporary Gathering Words (Jeremiah 8)
When the heart is sick and grief is deep,
Christ comforts us and calls us by name.
When life is hard and the road is long,
Christ leads us and guides us in love.
Welcome to the household of love!

Call to Worship (Jeremiah 8, Psalm 79)
Come to listen. Come to learn.
We come to worship and praise.
Come to remember. Come to reflect.
We come to hear God's word.
Come to cry out. Come to rejoice.
We come to sing and pray.

Opening Prayer (1 Timothy 2, Luke 16)
Savior God, welcome us into your household,
that we may bathe in the light of your grace.
Inspire us with your word,
that we may rejoice in the glory of your ways.
Strengthen us with your Spirit,
that we may go forth to serve you,
with passion and purpose,
in all that we say, and in all that we do.

Proclamation and Response

Prayer of Confession (Psalm 79, 1 Timothy 2)
How long will rage burn in our hearts?
How long will wrath consume our lives?
Wash over us with your grace, O God,
that our hearts may burn with your love.

Shower us with your mercy,
that we may welcome your forgiveness,
and spread your grace.
Redeem us in Christ Jesus,
that we may return to you,
restored and wholly yours.
In Christ's gracious name, we pray. Amen.
—Or—

Prayer of Confession (Luke 16)
Forgive us when we squander your gifts
and misuse our talents.
Forgive us when we protect our self-interests
and neglect the needs of the world.
Forgive us when we act cleverly for our personal gain,
and refuse to use our energies to help others.
Return us to you, Holy One,
and heal our hearts with your wisdom and love.
In Christ's name, we pray. Amen.

Words of Assurance (Jeremiah 8, 1 Timothy 2)
There is a balm in Gilead: Christ Jesus,
who has ransomed us with love and grace.
In the balm of Christ's love,
we are forgiven and restored to life.

Passing the Peace of Christ (1 Timothy 2, Luke 16)
Share signs of peace and love, that all may find here a
peaceful home of welcoming love.

Introduction to the Word (Jeremiah 8, 1 Timothy 2)
God's word may be the balm we most need. Listen for
God's truth, that you may find the balm of faith and
love.

Response to the Word (1 Timothy 2, Luke 16)
> We pray for leaders who need your wisdom.
> We pray for followers who need your guidance.
> We pray for seekers who need your presence.
> We pray for sinners who need your mercy.
> We pray for ourselves,
>> that we may be faithful
>>> in things both big and small,
>>> and that our actions and words
>>>> may be in service to you
>>>>> and your message of selfless love.
> In your gracious name, we pray. Amen.

Thanksgiving and Communion

Invitation to the Offering (Luke 16)
> The wealth of this world is not our own. The gifts of our lives are not our own. We are but stewards, granted the opportunity to share these gifts in service to God. Come, let us share in faithfulness and love.

Offering Prayer (Jeremiah 8, Luke 16)
> Pour out your Holy Spirit,
>> and bless the gifts we return to you now.
> May they be as soothing ointment
>> for a hurting and broken world.
> Bless the gifts of our lives,
>> and inspire us to be clever and creative,
>>> as we share generously and give abundantly,
>>>> the bounty we have received.
> In faithfulness and gratitude, we pray. Amen.

Sending Forth

Benediction (1 Timothy 2, Luke 16)
　　Go in peace.
　　Go in love.
　　Go in faithfulness to serve God
　　　　in all that you say,
　　　　and in all that you do.

September 25, 2016

Nineteenth Sunday after Pentecost, Proper 21
Mary Petrina Boyd

Color

Green

Scripture Readings

Jeremiah 32:1-3a, 6-15; Psalm 91:1-6, 14-16;
1 Timothy 6:6-19; Luke 16:19-31

Theme Ideas

Money is a topic of several scriptures, but is treated in
different ways. God told Jeremiah to make a foolish in-
vestment that would be a sign of hope for tomorrow.
Luke contrasts the fate of the wealthy man, who ignored
the needy, with that of the poor man, Lazarus. Paul's letter to Timothy warns about the dangers of money with
the familiar phrase: "The love of money is the root of all
kinds of evil" (v. 10). Today's scriptures call us to trust
God rather than wealth and our own efforts—for God
is the One who protects and sustains us, and who provides all that we need.

Invitation and Gathering

Contemporary Gathering Words (Psalm 91)
Don't be afraid in the night—
    God is watching over us.
Don't worry as the day breaks—
    God is with us.
Don't be concerned in the middle of the day—
    God takes care of us.
Don't fret as the day ends—
    God is still beside us.
In every moment, God is there!

Call to Worship (Psalm 91, 1 Timothy 6)
God is our refuge and stronghold.
    We will place our trust in God.
God's faithful love protects us.
    We will not be afraid.
When times are troubling,
    God will be with us.
When we cry out,
    God will answer us.
Through the years of our lives,
God is with us.
We look to the future with hope,
for God is our solid foundation.

Opening Prayer (Psalm 91, 1 Timothy 6, Luke 16)
God, you are wrapped in mystery, shrouded with light,
    unseen, but ever with us.
Yet, you care for us—
    keeping us safe, protecting us,
        and answering us when we call.

It is easy to cling to our bank accounts,
    and place our trust in our possessions,
        but they are not what really matters.
You are the true riches in our lives.
Open our hearts to one another
    and to the needs of the world,
        that we may share your abundance,
           and find true life in your love.
Our hope is in you,
    source of goodness and life. Amen.

Proclamation and Response

Prayer of Confession (Jeremiah 32, Psalm 91, 1 Timothy 6, Luke 16)

Ever-present God, we find so much to worry about.
The world seems a scary place,
    filled with violence and destruction.
Things seem to be coming apart
    and we don't know what the future holds.
Trying so hard to control what is happening to us,
    we look to our savings accounts for security.
Our possessions take so much energy and focus
    that we ignore those in need,
        even when they are right in front of us.
Help us place our trust in you, O God.
Remind us of your continuing care for all creation.
Teach us to see the needs of the world
        and to respond with care and compassion,
           that we may be faithful, gentle, loving people.
Amen.

Words of Assurance (1 Timothy 6)
>   Put your hope in God,
>   who richly provides for our needs.
>   Enjoy God's good gifts
>   as you share what you have with others.
>   Delight in the treasures God provides.

Passing the Peace of Christ (Psalm 91)
>   We live secure, tucked under Gods wings like tiny
>   chicks. Reach out to one another, sharing the deep peace
>   that comes from God's care for us. Let us offer Christ's
>   blessing to one another.

Prayer of Preparation (Jeremiah 32, 1 Peter 6)
>   Open our hearts to your word, O God.
>   Help us set aside all that separates us from you.
>   Turn us away from stupid and harmful passions.
>   Give us courage to hear your challenge for the future.
>   Amen

Response to the Word (1 Timothy 6)
>   Pursue righteousness.
>   Seek holy living.
>   Look for faithfulness.
>   Work to endure.
>   Follow gentleness.
>   Be a strong competitor in the good fight of faith.
>   Grab hold of God's ways—
>   ways that lead to abundant life.
>   Live in the light of God's love!

Thanksgiving and Communion

Invitation to the Offering (Luke 16, 1 Timothy 6)

The rich man asked Father Abraham to warn his brothers about the danger of depending on wealth and ignoring the needs of the world. We know we are called to use all that God gives us to care for one another. We are invited to be rich in the good things that we do, to share with others, and to be generous.

Offering Prayer (Psalm 91, 1 Timothy 6)

You alone are God—
> King of kings, Lord of lords—
>> living in eternal light.

Yet you care for us—
> protecting us in times of danger,
>> and giving us all that we need.

All that we have comes from you.
We bring you our gifts this day,
> that those in need may find food, clothing,
>> and shelter.

We commit ourselves to acts of goodness,
> generosity, and hospitality.

For we know that you are with us,
> and you walk with us into the future with hope.

Invitation to Communion (1 Timothy 6, Luke 16)

This is God's table. Here, all gather and are welcome. Both Lazarus and the rich man are invited to share in God's bounty. God has richly provided everything for our enjoyment. So come and gather here. Feast on Christ's love. Trust in God's care. Open yourself to the gifts of the Spirit. Then be ready to share that gift with others.

Sending Forth

Benediction (Psalm 91, 1 Timothy 6)
Pursue God's ways: Righteousness, holy living,
    faithfulness, love, endurance, and gentleness.
Share the abundance of God's gifts with others.
Remember that God is our refuge, the One we can trust.
No matter what, no matter when, God will be with you!

October 2, 2016

Twentieth Sunday after Pentecost, Proper 22
World Communion Sunday
Mary J. Scifres

Color

Green or White

Scripture Readings

Lamentations 1:1-6; Psalm 137; 2 Timothy 1:1-14;
Luke 17:5-10

Theme Ideas

Today's lections encourage us to revive and rekindle the
gifts that God's Spirit has given us. Whether suffering
in exile in need of God's strength and comfort, or growing a new community of faith in need of inspiration and
spiritual maturity, God gives us a spirit of courage to increase our faith and to fulfill Christ's call in our lives. By
constantly attending to this call and to the gifts given to
us, we are strengthened for the journey and empowered
to live as faithful disciples.

Invitation and Gathering

Contemporary Gathering Words (2 Timothy 1)
> God has called us together,
>> and so we gather as the body of Christ,
>> to revive our souls and strengthen our faith.
> God calls us as one body,
>> and so we gather in unity and love.
> God calls us to be disciples of Jesus Christ,
>> and so we gather to rekindle our calling
>> and empower our gifts to serve and love
>> in Christ's name.

Call to Worship (2 Timothy 1)
> The Spirit calls with power and strength.
> **Praise God for this gift of faith!**
> The Spirit welcomes us with mercy and love.
> **Praise God for this gift of grace!**

Opening Prayer (2 Timothy 1, Luke 17)
> Inspire us this day, O God.
> With the power of your Holy Spirit,
>> revive our courage.
> With Christ's holy calling in our lives,
>> rekindle our sense of purpose.
> With your steadfast love and faithfulness,
>> renew our faith.
> In gratitude and trust, we pray. Amen.

Proclamation and Response

Prayer of Confession (Lamentations 1, Psalm 137, 2 Timothy 1, Luke 17)
> Merciful God, comfort us when we wander into exile
> and find ourselves lost and alone.

Forgive us when we wander from your gracious love
    and find ourselves falling into sin.
In Christ Jesus, reconcile us to yourself,
    and bring us back into your loving embrace.
Revive our souls, strengthen our faith,
    and bless us with your holy calling,
        that we may be inspired to live your calling,
            and trust in your grace,
                all the days of our lives.
In Christ's mercy and grace, we pray. Amen.

Words of Assurance (2 Timothy 1)
God did not give us a spirit that is timid,
    but one that is powerful, loving, and self-controlled.
Trust in the power of this good news:
    God's grace is ours through Christ Jesus,
    who has destroyed both death and sin.
In the name of Christ, we are forgiven and made anew.

Prayer of Preparation (2 Timothy 1)
Spirit of God, call to us with your holy calling.
Inspire us with your powerful presence.
Strengthen our faith with your holy word.
In gratitude and trust, we pray. Amen.

Response to the Word or Invitation to Anointing
(2 Timothy 1)
Remember the faith of our mothers and fathers
    in Christian faith.
Trust in the strength that comes from the power
    of the Holy Spirit in our lives.
Revive your holy calling
    . as you receive the gift of anointing and prayer.

(Invite congregation forward for laying on of hands and anointing prayer in response to, or preparation for, Holy Communion.)

Thanksgiving and Communion

Invitation to the Offering or Offering Prayer (Psalm 137, 2 Timothy 1)

May these gifts bring hope to those who are despairing,
> comfort to those who are grieving,
>> nurture to those who are growing,
>>> and inspiration to those who are striving
>>>> to answer Christ's call.

The Great Thanksgiving

God be with you.
> **And also with you.**

Lift up your hearts.
> **We lift them up to God.**

Let us give thanks to the God of unity and love.
> **It is right to give God our thanks and praise.**

It is right, and a good and joyful thing,
> always and everywhere to give thanks to you,
> almighty God, creator of heaven and earth.

In the beginning, you swept across the earth
> with your Spirit of life and renewal.

From the earth's first gardens to mountaintop storms,
> you have spoken and called us into covenant
> to be your holy people.

When we wandered away and fell short of your call,
> you spoke yet again, calling us to walk in your ways.

From laws on tablets to warnings from prophets,
> you have spoken your truth

and renewed your covenant with us,
reviving our souls and rekindling our holy calling
with your grace and love.
And so, with your people on earth,
and all the company of heaven,
we praise your name
and join their unending hymn:
Holy, holy, holy One, God of power and might,
heaven and earth are full of your glory.
Hosanna in the highest. Blessed is the one
who comes in the name of God.
Hosanna in the highest.

Holy are you and blessed is your holy name.
In the fullness of time, you sent Christ Jesus
to call us to new life and renewed faith.
With a holy calling, Christ calls to us even now,
reviving our journey of discipleship
and strengthening our life of faith.
Through Christ's powerful love and endless grace,
we are invited into your presence,
rescued from our sins, and led on your path
of justice and righteousness.
In Christ's grace, you revive us and make us whole.
As children of your new covenant,
sealed by water and the Spirit,
we come to you now with joy and gratitude,
remembering how Jesus shared bread and wine,
renewing and reviving the lives of his friends,
his most faithful disciples,
even as they faced their deepest fears
and their greatest sins.

On the night before his death, Jesus took bread,
    gave thanks to you, broke the bread,
    gave it to the disciples, and said,
    "Take, eat; this is my body which is given for you.
    Do this in remembrance of me."
When the supper was over, Jesus took the cup,
    gave thanks to you, gave it to the disciples,
    and said, "Drink from this, all of you;
    this is my life in the new covenant, poured out
    for you and for many for the forgiveness of sins.
    Do this, as often as you drink it,
    in remembrance of me."

And so, in remembrance of these
    your life-giving acts of love and grace,
    we offer ourselves in praise and thanksgiving
    as children of your covenant,
    renewed and redeemed by your grace,
    in union with Christ's love for us,
    as we proclaim the mystery of faith.
    Christ has died.
    Christ is risen.
    Christ will come again.

Communion Prayer
    Pour out your Holy Spirit on us
        and on these gifts of bread and wine.
    Make them be for us the life and love of Christ,
        that we may be for the world the body of Christ,
            redeemed and revived by Christ's love
                and grace.
    By your Spirit, make us one with Christ,
        one with each other,

and one in ministry to all the world,
> until Christ comes in final victory
> > and we feast at his heavenly banquet.
Through Jesus Christ,
> with the Holy Spirit in your holy Church,
> > all honor and glory is yours, almighty God,
> > > now and forever more. Amen.

Giving the Bread and Cup
(The bread and wine are given to the people with these or other words of blessing.)
The life of Christ, reviving your body.
The love of Christ, renewing your soul.

Sending Forth

Benediction (2 Timothy 1)
In unity and love, we have gathered around the table.
In joy and hope, we have come to worship.
With strengthened faith, we go forth to love.
With our calling renewed, we go forth to serve.
—*Or*—

Benediction (2 Timothy 1)
With power and strength, the Spirit sends us forth
> to welcome and to serve with mercy and love.

October 9, 2016

Twenty-first Sunday after Pentecost, Proper 23
B. J. Beu

Color

Green

Scripture Readings

Jeremiah 29:1, 4-7; Psalm 66:1-12; 2 Timothy 2:8-15;
Luke 17:11-19

Theme Ideas

Suffering is a part of life. It's how we respond that is
the key. Do we give up, or do we push through? Do we
curse those who curse us, or do we seek their blessing?
Jeremiah tells the exiles in Babylon to build houses, plant
gardens, and pray for the welfare of the city where they
are held captive—for it is in the city's welfare that they
will find their welfare. The psalmist notes that God has
tested the people with fire and water, but has brought
them out to a spacious place. The proper response to
such grace is worship and praise. Paul tells Timothy that
while he is chained for the gospel, the word of God is
not, and that he embraces his suffering gladly for the

sake of God's elect. After healing ten lepers, Jesus re-marks that only one leper is truly made well—for only one returned to give thanks. Suffering happens. That's life. But how we respond to that suffering makes all the difference in the world.

Invitation and Gathering

Contemporary Gathering Words (Jeremiah 29, Luke 17)
Where are you on your journey with God? Have you wandered far away? Are you stuck in the past? Have you lost hope for the future? Do not despair. Build hous-es of joy. Plant gardens of faith. Offer thanks and praise to the living God, and you will be made well.

Call to Worship (Psalm 66, Luke 17)
Make a joyful noise to God.
Sing God's praises.
God has led us through fire and water,
and laid burdens on our backs.
But now God has led us out
into a spacious place.
Rejoice in the Lord.
Shout the glories of our God.
Let us worship in gratitude and praise this day.

Opening Prayer (Jeremiah 29, 2 Timothy 2, Luke 17)
Author of hope and renewal,
though our bodies grow weak
and our spirits faint within us,
your word is not chained,
but leads us ever forward.

Teach us to bloom where we are planted
and to pray for the welfare of all,
that our hope may be kindled
and our faith may be strengthened.
In gratitude and deep joy, we pray. Amen.

Proclamation and Response

Prayer of Confession (Jeremiah 29, Psalm 66, Luke 17:19)
Elusive One,
why do you test us so?
You have brought us into the net,
and laid burdens on our backs.
You have tried us like silver,
and refined us like gold.
You have led us through fire and water,
and let others ride over our heads.
But it was you who brought us through
to a good and spacious place.
Has this just been some kind of test,
some character building exercise?
We do not understand your ways, Holy One,
yet we will praise your name—
for you are our hope, and our deliverer.
Give us the faith to put our trust in you,
that we may hear the words of Jesus:
"Your faith has healed you." Amen.

Words of Assurance (2 Timothy 2:11-12a)
Hear these words of assurance from Paul:
If we have died with Christ,
we will also live with him.
And if we endure with Christ,
we will also reign with him.

Passing the Peace of Christ (Jeremiah 29)
> Seek the welfare of this place and its people. Share signs
> of love and peace, as you greet and pray for your neigh-
> bor this day. In this we flower as God's people.
> (Mary J. Scifres)

Introduction to the Word (2 Timothy 2)
> Paul reminds Timothy that the word of God is not
> chained. Listen for that word—for it is a healing word
> that proclaims grace and love.

Response to the Word (2 Timothy 2, Luke 17)
> Let us be more than hearers only,
>> but doers of the word.
> Let us present ourselves to the world,
>> and show what God has done for us.
> Let us present ourselves to God,
>> and offer ourselves as disciples of Christ,
>>> approved by the power of the Holy Spirit,
>>>> to share the word of truth with the world.

Thanksgiving and Communion

Invitation to the Offering (Jeremiah 29)
> Even in exile, God instructed the people to seek the
> welfare of the city where they were forced to call home.
> Even among strangers and captors, our welfare is tied
> to the welfare of others. Let us give generously, that we
> may plant the love of God all around us, through the
> ministry and mission of this church.

Offering Prayer (Psalm 66, Luke 17)
> Almighty God,
>> we are witnesses of your love and grace.

Your power is a wonder to behold.
For the healing in our lives,
 we thank you.
For the power of your Spirit within us,
 we praise you.
Receive these gifts
 as signs of our thanks and praise.
Receive our very lives,
 for we are your servants,
 and you are our God. Amen.

Sending Forth

Benediction (Jeremiah 29, Luke 17)
Sow seeds of faith and hope,
and bloom where you are planted.
 We will care for our neighbors,
 and bear the fruit of kindness and compassion.
Grow with the power of God's Spirit,
and bloom with the love of Christ.
 We will offer Christ's mercy,
 and help a hurting world be made well.

October 16, 2016

Twenty-second Sunday after Pentecost, Proper 24
Mary J. Scifres
[Copyright © 2015 by Mary J. Scifres. Used by permission.]

Color

Green

Scripture Readings

Jeremiah 31:27-34; Psalm 119:97-104; 2 Timothy 3:14–4:5;
Luke 18:1-8

Theme Ideas

The theme of God's guidance emerges from today's
scriptures. Such guidance may come through scripture,
through prayer, or through the spiritual wisdom we
gain on our journeys of faith. God's wisdom is imprint-
ed on our hearts in the form of love's law—a law that
guides our paths and strengthens our faith.

Invitation and Gathering

Contemporary Gathering Words (Jeremiah 31)
  Guided by God, we gather to listen for truth and to discern
  the Spirit's wisdom. As we plant gardens of kindness,

we discover that God has already planted love in our hearts. As we build houses of love, we realize that Christ is creating new life in our souls.

Call to Worship (Psalm 119)
God's teachings are sweeter than honey.
Christ's love is more precious than jewels.
The Spirit's wisdom is mightier than the sword.
God's guidance is the treasure we seek.

Opening Prayer (Psalm 119, 2 Timothy 3–4)
God of discernment and truth,
    guide us as we listen for your wisdom.
Guide our hearts,
    that we may receive your love.
Guide our minds,
    that we may accept your challenges.
Guide our lives,
    that we may follow your direction.
Guide us with your wisdom and truth.

Proclamation and Response

Prayer of Confession (Psalm 119, 2 Timothy 3–4)
Forgive us, O God, when we reject your teaching,
    and neglect your law.
Forgive us when we meditate on movies and gossip,
    and ignore your words of love and compassion.
Forgive us when we pursue power and wealth,
    and forsake the path of justice and mercy.
Guide us back to you,
    that we may walk in your ways
        and live in your love.
In Christ's grace and mercy, we pray. Amen.

Words of Assurance (Jeremiah 31)
    In the new covenant of Christ Jesus,
        grace and forgiveness are ours.
    Thanks be to God!

Passing the Peace of Christ (2 Timothy 4)
    As we encourage one another with signs of peace and
    words of love, let us share in the peace of Christ.

Prayer of Preparation (Psalm 119)
    How we love your instruction, O God!
    We think about it constantly,
        knowing that your teachings
            will make us wiser and more understanding
                than we can possibly imagine.
    Your word is pleasing to the ear,
        and your love is sweeter than honey.
    Help us listen for your nourishing word,
        that we may receive your guidance this day. Amen.

Response to the Word (Psalm 119)
    We love your law, O God,
        and we yearn for your wisdom
            to be written upon our hearts,
                that we might infuse this world
                    with your love.
    Imprint us with hope,
        strengthen us with perseverance,
            and guide us with compassion.
    In Christ's name, we pray. Amen.

Thanksgiving and Communion

Offering Prayer (Jeremiah 31, Psalm 119)
    May our gifts become instruments of your truth,
        and examples of your love.

Plant new hope with these gifts,
   and build a world of justice
      with the ministries we dedicate to you now.
In Christ's name, we pray. Amen.

Invitation to Communion (Jeremiah 31, Psalm 119)
   Come to the garden of grace.
   Come to the house of love.
   Come, for the gift of love
      is the most precious teaching of all.
   Come to the table, where all are welcome, all are fed,
      and none shall be afraid.

Sending Forth

Benediction (Jeremiah 31)
   Go and build houses of love.
   Go and plant gardens of kindness.
   Go and create lives of goodness.
   Go and proclaim the promise of justice.
   Go with the blessings of God.

October 23, 2016

Twenty-third Sunday after Pentecost, Proper 25
B. J. Beu
[Copyright © 2015 by B. J. Beu. Used by permission.]

Color

Green

Scripture Readings

Joel 2:23-32; Psalm 65; 2 Timothy 4:6-8, 16-18;
Luke 18:9-14

Theme Ideas

God enters into our struggles to bring us joy. In Joel, the
Israelites, who had suffered long years of drought, are
given life-giving rain. They also receive the promise of
prophecies, dreams, and visions. The psalmist rejoices
in the bounty of God's blessings. Even as Paul contem-
plates his martyrdom, he rejoices that he has finished the
race in faith and will receive the crown of righteousness.
In Luke, Jesus chastises those who build themselves up,
even as he offers forgiveness to those who humble themselves before God. God never abandons us, especially in
the worst of times. This is good news indeed.

Invitation and Gathering

Contemporary Gathering Words (Joel 2, Psalm 65, 2 Timothy 4)

God dreams and visions us into being. And so we dream God's dreams. And we vision God's visions. Let us not scorn our dreams and visions, for they are a holy gift.

Call to Worship (Joel 2, Psalm 65)

Rejoice in the Lord and be glad.
God is our hope and our salvation.
The Lord blesses the earth with rain.
God crowns the year with bounty.
The Lord silences the roaring seas.
God quiets the tumult of the people.
The Lord makes old men dream dreams.
God makes young girls see visions.
Rejoice in the Lord and be glad.
God is our hope and our salvation.

Opening Prayer (Joel 2, Psalm 65, 2 Timothy 4)

Giver of dreams and visions,
pour out your Spirit on all flesh,
for we long to feel your presence
in the tumult of our lives.
Show your portents in the heavens,
and your signs on the earth and seas,
that all may know to humble themselves
and dwell within your courts,
living in peace and harmony
with one another. Amen.

Proclamation and Response

Prayer of Confession (Joel 2, Psalm 65, 2 Timothy 4)
Merciful God,
you prepare us for the marathon of life,
but we act as if it were a sprint.
We are tired from fighting the good fight.
We are exhausted from running the race.
We are weary from keeping the faith.
Come to us once more, O God,
and speak your words of promise,
for we need your quiet center
to silence the tumult of our lives.
Bless us with prophesy,
revive our dreams,
and guide us with visions,
that we may stay strong until the end,
and receive your righteous crown. Amen.

Assurance of Pardon (2 Timothy 4)
In Christ, we share a crown of righteousness
with those who love him
and long for his appearance.
Rejoice and be glad!

Response to the Word (Ephesians 1, Acts 2)
Hold fast to the promises of God. God will pour out the Holy Spirit on all flesh. Our sons and our daughters shall prophesy. Our old men and women shall dream dreams. The young and old alike shall see visions. Hold fast to the promises of God, for they are good and true.

Thanksgiving and Communion

Offering Prayer (Psalm 65, Luke 18)
God of overflowing abundance,
    you water the earth with live-giving rain;
    you clothe the meadows with glorious flowers;
    you deck the valleys with grain;
    you crown the year with your bounty;
    you make the gateways of the evening
      and the morning shout for joy.
With what can we come before you
    to repay you for your many blessings?
Receive the fruit of our labor.
Receive also the gift of our humble thanks,
    that you may keep our hearts for safe keeping.
Amen.

Sending Forth

Benediction (2 Timothy 4)
Live well, that you may boldly proclaim:
    I have fought the good fight.
    I have finished the race.
    I have kept the faith.
Love deeply, that you may wear
    the crown of righteousness
    given to all who love God
    and yearn for Christ's appearing.

October 30, 2016

Twenty-fourth Sunday after Pentecost, Proper 26
Reformation Sunday
Laura Jaquith Bartlett

Color

Green

Scripture Readings

Habakkuk 1:1-4; 2:1-4; Psalm 119:137-144;
2 Thessalonians 1:1-4, 11-12; Luke 19:1-10

Alternate Scripture Readings for All Saints Sunday
Daniel 7:1-3, 15-18; Psalm 149; Ephesians 1:11-23;
Luke 6:20-31
(See online supplemental materials for All Saints Sunday.)

Theme Ideas

Habakkuk is frustrated by the violence, strife, conflict, and anguish all around him. Hmmm, sounds a lot like life in the twenty-first century. The prophet wants God to do something about this injustice right now! According to Habakkuk, justice doesn't stand a chance with all these wicked people around. And then we have Luke, sharing a story of a "wicked" person who meets

Jesus...and repents! The Church's job is not to stay safely inside our sterile, holy sanctuaries, free of conflict and anguish; it is to engage the world where wickedness and injustice live, where an encounter with Jesus offers much-needed transformation. Such life is not trouble-free, as 2 Thessalonians points out. But that is precisely where faith grows, love increases, and thanksgiving abounds.

Invitation and Gathering

Contemporary Gathering Words (2 Thessalonians 1)
To the church of [*fill in the name of your church or community here*], which is in God, our Mother and Father, and in the Lord Jesus Christ, grace and peace to all of you!

Call to Worship (2 Thessalonians 1)
Greetings to you in the name of God.
Greetings to you!
Greetings to you in the name of Christ Jesus
and the Holy Spirit.
Greetings to one and all!
God gives us everything we need.
Thanks be to God!
Our God makes us everything we are to be.
Let us offer thanks to the Holy Three-in-One!

Opening Prayer (Habakkuk 1, Luke 19)
Dear God, it is so easy to get discouraged
by the news in our community,
across our country, and around the globe.
Everywhere we look, we hear of violence,
conflict, and injustice.

Like the prophets of old, we want to cry out:
    "Hurry up and change the world, God!"
And then we look at our own lives
    and realize you are calling us
        to hurry up and change the world.
As we encounter Christ in our worship this hour,
    may our live be transformed;
        may we leave this place eager to share
            your blessings, your justice, and your love
                with a world yearning for a new way
                    of living.
Amen.

Proclamation and Response

Prayer of Confession (Luke 19, Habakkuk 1)
    The bulletin tells us it's time
    for the Prayer of Confession,
        but is that unnecessary here in this church?
    We are not Zacchaeus.
    We don't cheat others.
    What do we have to confess?
        God, we live in a world
            where our systems, corporations,
                and institutions oppress others.
        Forgive us when we keep silent.
    We don't perpetrate violence against others.
    We are a community of love.
    What do we have to confess?
        God, we live in a broken world
            that practices violence
                in response to conflict.
        Forgive us when we keep silent.
    We are a community of good people
        who worship Christ and show love and mercy.

What do we have to confess?
God, each and every week, we show ourselves
to be imperfect human beings,—
we miss opportunities to say thank you;
we take others for granted;
we omit the whole truth in conversations;
we snap at family and loved ones;
we participate in gossip;
we neglect to express gratitude to you
for your many blessings.
Forgive us when we accept our shortcomings
and fail to come to you for help.
(Allow a time of silence.)

Words of Assurance (Luke 19)
Salvation came to Zacchaeus, a cheater and a thief.
Today, salvation comes us in the person of Jesus Christ,
who forgives us and sets us free,
that we may be transformed in holy love.

Passing the Peace of Christ (Luke 19)
Has your life been changed by an encounter with Jesus
Christ? As you greet those around you, share with them
the opportunity for transformation that is available
through Christ's peace and love.

Introduction to the Word (Habakkuk 1, Luke 19)
(This dialogue for two people is meant to follow the Habakkuk
reading and to precede the Luke reading.)

One: *(looking up from reading a newspaper)* I don't
know what this world is coming to! I sure
wish we could go back to the good old days
when you could leave your doors unlocked
and we didn't need to have metal detectors
in schools.

Two: *You mean go back to ancient times and all the violence, anguish, conflict, devastation, and wickedness we just heard about?*

One: Okay, okay, I get your point. Maybe the good old days never existed. Maybe the world has always been a terrible place. Is that supposed to make me feel better?

Two: *That's not exactly my point! Sure, there's always been wickedness in the world, but God has a different idea for us. God never gives up on the world, no matter what we do.*

One: I don't know…we seem to be really messing things up these days.

Two: *Speaking of the Bible, there was somebody else a long time ago who had messed things up pretty badly. Listen to what happened when this guy had an encounter with Jesus.*

Response to the Word or Benediction (Habakkuk 1, Luke 19)

There is violence in our world,
but Christ shows us the way of peace.
We will go in peace.
There is wickedness in our world,
but Christ offers us hope and compassion.
We will go to be Christ's hope.
There is hatred in our world,
but Christ teaches us how to love.
We will go to share God's love.
There is brokenness in our lives,
but Christ opens the door to repentance.
**We will go as transformed people
to change the world.**

Thanksgiving and Communion

Offering Prayer (2 Thessalonians, Luke 19)
God of amazing grace,
    you have given us everything,
        including our very lives.
Though we cannot earn your love,
    you give it to us freely.
And so we thank you.
Receive our gifts,
    as expressions of our thanksgiving and praise,
        and our commitment to live as you intend.
We pray in the name of the one
    who offers salvation to all, Jesus Christ. Amen.

Sending Forth

Benediction (2 Thessalonians, The Message)
In the name of God, our Mother and Father,
    who gives us everything we need...
In the name of Christ Jesus, our Master,
    whose love transforms us...
In the name of the Holy Spirit,
    whose power strengthens our faith
    and increases our love...
Let us go in peace.
Let us go with God.
Let us go to transform the world. Amen.

November 6, 2016

Twenty-fifth Sunday after Pentecost, Proper 27
Deborah Sokolove

Color

Green

Scripture Readings

Haggai 1:15b–2:9; Psalm 145:1-5, 17-21;
2 Thessalonians 2:1-5, 13-17; Luke 20:27-38

Theme Ideas

The promise of love and grace that God gave to our ancestors is given to all who love and bless God's holy name. Even when we live in challenging times, even when we are afraid or in pain, God comforts us and gives us strength whenever we ask. The living God is the God of the living, not the dead.

Invitation and Gathering

Contemporary Gathering Words (Psalm 145)
Let our mouths speak the praise of God.
Let us bless God's holy name forever and ever.
—*Or*—

Contemporary Gathering Words (Psalm 145)
Great is our God, and worthy of our praise. How can we stop our lips from singing of God's mighty deeds? How can we stop our hearts from rejoicing in God's glory as the morning dawns? Great is our God, and worthy of our praise.
(B. J. Beu)

Call to Worship (Haggai 1–2, Psalm 145)
Take courage, all you people.
Take courage, says the Holy One,
for I am with you.
Do not be afraid, for God's Spirit is with us.
The Holy One watches over all who come in love.
Let our mouths speak the praise of God.
Let us bless God's holy name forever and ever.

Opening Prayer (Psalm 145, 2 Thessalonians 2, Luke 20)
Blessed are you, Holy One, our God.
You watch over all who love you,
and are near to all who call on your name.
You are the God of the living,
calling us to bring the good news
of your grace and love:
to a world that lives in fear of destruction,
to a world that that is filled with heartache
and pain.
As we gather to praise and bless you,
fill us with your Spirit,
and give us the courage to be your people,
the body of Christ.
This we pray, in Jesus' name, who died and rose,
and lives in us and through us. Amen.

Proclamation and Response

Prayer of Confession (Haggai 1–2, Psalm 145, Luke 20)
Blessed are you, Holy One, our God.
You call us to speak your praises,
to let all the world know
that you are great and mighty.
Yet, we are silent when people say
there is no God.
We are afraid to let them know
what we believe.
You call us to bring good news to the brokenhearted,
and to be your living body
to a broken and hurting world.
Yet, we are afraid to claim
your promise of grace,
filled as we are with despair
at the problems we see around us.
Forgive us when we forget your promise
to bring justice and kindness.
Forgive us when we are neither just nor kind.

Words of Assurance (Psalm 145)
When we call on God in truth and love,
God hears our cry and saves us.
In the name of Christ, you are forgiven.
In the name of Christ, you are forgiven.
Glory to God. Amen.

Passing the Peace of Christ (Psalm 145, 2 Thessalonians 2)
As forgiven and loved members of Christ's body, let us
share signs of peace with one another.
The peace of Christ be with you.
The Peace of Christ be with you always.

Response to the Word (2 Thessalonians 2, Luke 20)
Gracious, loving, comforting God,
you are the God of the living—
in you, all who have gone before us in faith
are alive.
**Help us so to live, that we, too, may live in you,
and that you may live in us. Amen.**

Thanksgiving and Communion

Offering Prayer (2 Thessalonians 2, Luke 20)
Living, loving, gracious God,
in you we find eternal life.
**Accept these gifts,
that we may spread the good news
of your comfort and grace
throughout the world.**

Great Thanksgiving
Christ be with you.
And also with you.
Lift up your hearts.
We lift them up to God.
Let us give our thanks to the Holy One.
It is right to give our thanks and praise.

It is a right, good, and a joyful thing,
always and everywhere, to give our thanks to you,
who brought your people out of Egypt,
brought the exiles from Babylon back to Jerusalem,
and promised peace and eternal comfort
to all who love you.

And so, with your creatures on earth
    and all the heavenly chorus, we praise your name
    and join their unending hymn:
    Holy, holy, holy Lord, God of power and might,
        heaven and earth are full of your glory.
    Hosanna in the highest. Blessed is the one
        who comes in the name of the Lord.
    Hosanna in the highest.
Holy are you, and holy is your child, Jesus Christ,
    who reminded those who questioned him
    that the God of Abraham and Sarah,
    the God of Isaac and Rebecca,
    the God Jacob and Leah and Rachel,
    is the God of the living, not the dead,
    and that all who love God have eternal life.

On the night in which he gave himself up,
    Jesus took bread, gave thanks to you,
    broke the bread, and gave it to the disciples, saying:
    "Take, eat; this is my body which is given for you.
    Do this in remembrance of me."
When the supper was over, Jesus took the cup,
    offered thanks and gave it to the disciples, saying:
    "Drink from this, all of you;
    this is my life in the new covenant,
    poured out for you and for many,
    for the forgiveness of sins.
    Do this, as often as you drink it,
    in remembrance of me."
And so, in remembrance of your mighty acts
    in Jesus Christ, we proclaim the mystery of faith.
    Christ has died.
    Christ is risen.
    Christ will come again.

Pour out your Holy Spirit on our gathering,
 and on these gifts of bread and wine.
Make them be for us the body and blood of Christ,
 that we may be the body of Christ
 to a world that longs for peace.
To the Creator of all, Holy Spirit, and Christ Jesus—
 one God, living in us and through us
  and around us,
   we give you our thanks and praise.
Amen.

Sending Forth

Benediction (2 Thessalonians 2)
 In all things, give thanks to God,
  for you have been called to bear witness
  to the good news.
 And may the Creator of all, Holy Spirit,
  and Christ Jesus—one God,
  living in you and through you and around you,
  comfort your hearts and strengthen them
  in every good work and deed.
 Amen.

November 13, 2016

Twenty-sixth Sunday after Pentecost, Proper 28
Mary J. Scifres

Color

Green

Scripture Readings

Isaiah 65:17-25; Isaiah 12; 2 Thessalonians 3:6-13;
Luke 21:5-19

Theme Ideas

Change is in the air, not just at this time of year, but in to-day's scriptures. Isaiah promises a new creation, even as Luke warns of impending turmoil and the destruction of the temple. It seems that the church at Thessalonica has changed: Followers have become undisciplined and idle in their discipleship. The epistle calls them back to steadfast discipleship. Even in the face of change, we are called to rejoice in the new things that come from God and to be steadfast and faithful in doing "right" when other changes are not of God. The challenge to balance joy-filled and God-led change with steadfast faithful-ness offers interesting food for thought in designing worship and messages for these scriptures.

Invitation and Gathering

Contemporary Gathering Words (Isaiah 65, 1 Thessalonians 3)

> Look and listen! God is always creating us anew, offering new perspectives for living as faithful disciples. Look and listen! God is calling us to love God, love neighbor, and love ourselves. Look and listen, as new possibilities walk hand in hand with holy truth.

Call to Worship (Isaiah 65, Isaiah 12)

> Be glad and rejoice, for God is creating us ever new.
> **New peace, new love, new life—**
> **these are the promises of Christ.**
> Thank the Lord, and call upon God's name!
> **We will sing and shout with hope and joy,**
> **for God is with us here.**

Opening Prayer (Isaiah 65, Isaiah 12, 1 Thessalonians 3, Luke 21)

> Call upon us this day, Holy One of Israel.
> Be our Strength and Shield,
> > that we may be your steadfast followers,
> > > even as you mold us to be courageous prophets
> > > of change and hope.
> Be our Guide and our Shepherd,
> > that we may walk this challenging journey,
> > > open to your new creation,
> > > > even as we remain true to your calling
> > > > and your teaching in our lives.

Proclamation and Response

Prayer of Confession (Isaiah 65, Isaiah 12)

> Forgive us, gracious God,

when we do not trust your new creation
   or live up to your calling.
Give us the courage to face the changes you send
   and the new opportunities you offer.
Give us the confidence to trust your promises
   of peace and life.
Give us the strength to be instruments of your promises.
Give us the peace to be at home
   with both the wolves and the lambs in our midst.
Give us the hope to build your world,
   even when we fear the future,
      that we may be your new creation
         and your loving presence upon this earth.
In the name of Christ Jesus,
   who brought new life out of death, we pray. Amen.

Words of Assurance (Isaiah 65)

Look! God is creating a new heaven and a new earth.
Past events aren't remembered;
   they don't even come to mind.
In Christ Jesus, we're forgiven and made new.
Thanks be to God!

Passing the Peace of Christ (Isaiah 65)

As people of peace, let us share words of grace and gestures of love, as we pass the peace of Christ together.

Introduction to the Word (Luke 21)

Christ offers us words and wisdom, speaking from ancient times into God's ever growing future. Hold fast to this ancient wisdom, even as you listen for new words of challenge, for God is still speaking. Listen and you will live.

Response to the Word (Isaiah 65, 2 Thessalonians 3)
Let us pray for the new creation
God yearns to bring forth.
    God envisions a new creation,
    a world of peace and love...
A world where babies and old people are fed and loved,
nurtured and protected.
    God envisions a new creation,
    a world of hope and joy...
A world where houses are built and gardens are planted,
that all may have homes and be fed.
    God envisions a new church,
    a church of Christian love...
A church where followers are steadfast in love,
never wearying and never discouraged,
but always faithful in trust and hope.
    Mighty God, may we become your new creation,
        your new church, your body of Christ,
            bringing new hope to our world.
    In Christ's holy name, we pray. Amen.

Thanksgiving and Communion

Invitation to the Offering (2 Thessalonians 3)
Sisters and brothers, don't get discouraged from doing
what is right. It is a right and a good and joyful thing,
always and everywhere, to give thanks and to return
thanks by giving of ourselves and our worldly goods. In
this time of offering, let us work quietly and generously,
as we participate in the creation of a new heaven and
a new earth, through the offering of our gifts and the
giving of our lives.

Offering Prayer (Isaiah 12, Isaiah 65)
We thank you, God, for being our strength and shield,
    our salvation and our hope.
As we have drawn joy
    from the springs of your salvation,
        may these gifts become springs of hope
            to a world thirsty with need.
Empower our lives and our gifts,
    that we may become instruments
        of your new creation upon this earth.
In the name of our Creator God, we pray. Amen.

Sending Forth

Benediction (Isaiah 65)
Behold, you are a new creation in Christ Jesus!
    We rejoice and are glad,
    for God is making everything new!
Look! The world needs this hope!
    We go forth to proclaim God's new creation,
    as we live in peace and grow in love.

November 20, 2016

Reign of Christ / Christ the King Sunday
B. J. Beu

Color

White

Scripture Readings

Jeremiah 23:1-6; Luke 1:68-79; Colossians 1:11-20;
Luke 23:33-43

Theme Ideas

Today's scripture readings focus on themes of rescue
and light. Those responsible for shepherding God's
people have failed in their duties—a failure so complete
that the shepherds have actually scattered the sheep
and destroyed the flock. God promises to save a rem-
nant of the flock and raise up a righteous king who will
lead wisely and execute justice and righteousness in the
land. Christians proclaim Jesus as the righteous branch
promised in Jeremiah, and the prophet of the Most High
witnessed to in Luke. Christ is our true King—the Good
Shepherd who leads God's flock into fullness of life.

Invitation and Gathering

Contemporary Gathering Words (Jeremiah 23, Luke 1, Luke 23)

> Who will lead us with love and mercy? Who will execute justice and uphold righteousness in the land? Look to the Prince of Peace—who welcomes strangers, forgives criminals, and shines the light of God's love into the darkness of our world.

Call to Worship (Luke 1, Colossians 1, Luke 23)

> By the tender mercy of God,
> dawn is breaking, light has come.
> > **Blessed be the Lord.**
> By the gracious care of our Shepherd,
> the scattered are gathered, the lost are found.
> > **Holy is our God.**
> By the loving reign of the Prince of Peace,
> the weak are strengthened, the destroyer flees.
> > **Gentle is our King.**

Opening Prayer (Jeremiah 23, Luke 1, Colossians 1)

> King of glory,
> > as you shine your light
> > > into the darkness of our lives,
> > > > guide our feet in the way of peace;
> > as you shepherd your people,
> > > gather the lost and the scattered
> > > > into the safety of your flock.
> Reign in our hearts,
> > as you do in the heavens,
> > > that we may endure the struggles of this world
> > > > with patience and fortitude.
> In the light of your radiant love, we pray. Amen.

Proclamation and Response

Prayer of Confession (Jeremiah 23, Colossians 1, Luke 23)
Good Shepherd,
    the sheep of your pasture
      long to hear your voice;
    the sheep of your fold
      yearn to feel your gentle touch.
Other shepherds have scattered us,
    but we have willingly followed their call.
Other voices have led us astray,
    but we have eagerly heeded their false promises.
Strengthen us in our weakness
    with your glorious power,
      and gather us in through your mercy and grace,
        that we may be guided in the way of peace,
          through the power of your Holy Spirit.

Words of Assurance (Jeremiah 23, Luke 23:43)
Dying on the cross, Jesus told the prisoner beside him:
    "I assure you that today you will be with me
    in paradise."
Jesus does more than remember us,
    he gathers us to him as a shepherd gathers his flock.
Rejoice and be glad.

Passing the Peace of Christ (Luke 1)
Christ guides our feet in the way of peace. Let us share this peace as we greet one another this morning.

Introduction to the Word (Luke 1)
Christ shines light into the darkness of our world, and guides our feet in the way of peace. Listen for the word of God, that we may walk in the light of peace.

Response to the Word (Luke 1, Colossians 1)
>Christ has made us strong
>>through his glorious power.
>
>As Christ's light breaks forth,
>>God's saints are made to live
>>in a new and radiant dawn.
>
>Rejoice and be glad,
>>for Christ will guide our feet
>>in the way of peace.

Thanksgiving and Communion

Offering Prayer (Jeremiah 23)
>Loving Shepherd,
>>just as you gathered the lost and scattered sheep,
>>>that they might be fruitful and multiply,
>>>>gather our offerings this day,
>>>>>that they might multiply as they go forth
>>>>>to help a lost and scattered world.

Sending Forth

Benediction (Luke 1, Colossians 1, Luke 23)
>Draw strength from the power of the Lord.
>Draw courage from the patience and joy of the saints.
>Draw hope from the saving power of Christ's love.
>Go with the peace of the Lord.

November 24, 2016

Thanksgiving Day
Bill Hoppe

Color

Red

Scripture Readings

Deuteronomy 26:1-11; Psalm 100; Philippians 4:4-9;
John 6:25-35

Theme Ideas

God is gracious, selfless, giving, faithful, steadfast, constant, generous, nurturing, and loving. The Lord is all of
these things and so much more. How can we comprehend
a power so immense and indescribable that it can bring
an entire universe into being with a single command?
How can we comprehend this same power at work in
our individual lives, giving us the assurance that we are
loved and cared for? We can respond as God's people
and offer our unending and undying thanksgiving.

Invitation and Gathering

Contemporary Gathering Words (John 6)
Have we come here this day seeking satisfaction for
ourselves, or have we come seeking the creator and the

giver of all good things? Have we come here seeking our immediate needs, or have we come seeking lasting sustenance? Temporal or eternal, perishable or lasting— what have we come for? We have come to partake of the bread of life and the living water. We have come to thank Christ that our hunger and thirst are forever satisfied.

Call to Worship (Psalm 100, Philippians 4)

Rejoice in the Lord always!

Again, I say rejoice!

Our Lord is good, and we are God's people!

God's steadfast love is eternal!

We will enter the gates of the Lord
with praise and thanksgiving!

Give thanks to the Lord!

Bless God's holy name!

Rejoice in the Lord always!

Again, I say rejoice!

Opening Prayer (Deuteronomy 26, Psalm 100, John 6)

Gracious Lord, creator of all, giver of life,
> we praise you!

We worship you in humility and gratitude.

Surrounded by your love and care—
> we live and breathe,
> we laugh and cry,
> we labor and rest.

When our souls faint within us,
> you satisfy our hunger with the bread of life,
>> and satisfy our thirst with living water.

With joy and thanksgiving,
> we celebrate the unselfish bounty
>> you have bestowed upon us! Amen!

Proclamation and Response

Prayer of Confession (Deuteronomy 26, Psalm 100, Philippians 4, John 6)
> Lord, your selfless generosity
> > provides all that the world needs,
> > > yet we often keep your gifts for ourselves.
> Forgive us when we are thankless and indifferent
> > to the needs of others.
> Rather than open our mouths in praise or song,
> > we keep silent.
> We forget how deeply you care for us,
> > and we're blind to the abundance
> > > that surrounds us.
> Restore us, renew us,
> > and fill our hearts again with your love.
> Show us what it means to be truly grateful,
> > and return us to your presence. Amen.

Words of Assurance (Deuteronomy 26, Psalm 100, Philippians 4)
> In times of famine and plenty, the Lord is constant.
> God sustains us and gives us the things we need.
> Our prayers and pleadings are heard.
> The Lord is near: God is present with us.
> The indescribable peace of the Spirit enfolds us.
> All that is good, true, pure, noble, gracious,
> > lovable, and praiseworthy—
> > > this is what God has done for us.
> Thanks be to God.

Response to the Word (Deuteronomy 26, John 6)
> With arms opened wide and signs of wonders,
> > you have brought us to your side—

a place filled with more
  than we could ever want or need.
We find ourselves in a land
  flowing with milk and honey.
How can we not believe all you have told us?
How can we not trust all you have shown us?
We will follow the one you sent to guide us,
  the bread of life come down from heaven,
    the one who gives life to the world.
Lord, give us this bread always.
In your name, we pray. Amen.

Thanksgiving and Communion

Offering Prayer (Deuteronomy 26, Psalm 100)
Lord, we were born with nothing
  but the breath you breathed into us.
All that we have become,
  all that we have created,
    and all that we have worked for;
      all this was made possible through you.
We return what you have given to us
  as an offering of our thankfulness,
    and as a celebration of your love.
Gracious Creator, to you we offer our worship
  and our praise! Amen!

Sending Forth

Benediction (Psalm 100, Philippians 4)
Beloved, know that the Lord is God.
It is the Lord who made us.

We are God's people.
All that is true, all that is wonderful,
   all that is just and pure,
   all that is good and beautiful and right—
      all of this is a magnificent and indescribable gift.
Think about these things!
Keep doing the things you have learned and received,
   the things you have heard and seen,
      and the God of peace will be with you!
Amen and amen!

Meditation (Philippians 4:8)
"Think On These Things"

Music & Lyrics by Bill Hoppe & Rick Conklin
Copyright © 2006 by names of copyright owners.
Used by permission. All rights reserved.
From the album *Blaze Away*, by BrokenWorks
Released January 1, 2009
theband.brokenworks.com

We're more, much more
Than what we think
And yet, on thoughts
We rise or sink
For thoughts determine
Where we find our wings
Upon the winds of what life brings

So whatever is good, whatever is pure
Whatever gives off the brightest light
Whatever is real, whatever is true
Whatever is beautiful and right
Will spill into our lives and fill our dreams
Whenever we think on these things

And the peace of God we come to find
Will guard our hearts and our minds
When our gentleness begins to flow
To everyone, we'll start to show
The power of these thoughts we hold
And watch the promises unfold

All that's right, all that's pure
All that's good, all that's sure
All that's true, all that's fine
All the best, all the time
All that's fair, all we trust
All that's kind, all that's just
Whatever is beautiful and right

November 27, 2016

First Sunday of Advent (Year A)
Karin Ellis

Color

Purple

Scripture Readings

Isaiah 2:1-5; Psalm 122; Romans 13:11-14;
Matthew 24:36-44

Theme Ideas

Today's scriptures help us prepare our hearts and minds
for the arrival of God's Son. Isaiah lays before us a beautiful image of people from across the world gathering at
the mountain of the Lord, the house of God. Here they
will lay aside their weapons and learn to live in the light
of God. How will we keep the light burning this Advent
season? One way is to pray with the psalmist for peace.
Another way, suggested in Romans, is to carry the light
with us as we follow the ways of Jesus Christ. Matthew
reminds us that it is always good to be ready, for we never know when a guest might appear on our doorstep. Let
us walk in the light, and get our house ready, in order to
welcome the Christ child when he finally comes.

Invitation and Gathering

Contemporary Gathering Words (Psalm 122, Romans 13)

A light shines in the darkness. A prayer for peace is uttered in the silence. God's people gather to wait with hope.

Call to Worship (Isaiah 2, Psalm 122, Romans 13)

It is a joy to enter the house of the Lord!
Here we lay aside our differences
and pray for one another.
Here we catch a glimpse of light,
a promise of hope and new life.
Here we wait for the birth of the one
who will teach us how to love and serve.
It is a joy to enter the house of the Lord!
Come and praise God!

Opening Prayer (Isaiah 2, Psalm 122, Matthew 24)

God of hope, we come before you
full of expectation for what lies ahead.
We are excited about the birth of Christ,
but we know there is much to do
before this baby arrives.
A house needs to be prepared—
a house in our hearts,
where your grace may enter.
A people needs to pray—
a people longing for peace,
that reconciliation may take hold in our world.
A light needs to be turned on—
a light of holy love,
that we may reflect your glory.

God of new life,
    prepare our hearts and our lives,
        that we may wait with joy and hope
            for the birth of your Son. Amen.

Proclamation and Response

Prayer of Confession (Isaiah 2, Psalm 122, Romans 13, Matthew 24)
    Merciful God, how many times have we wandered?
    We spend our lives searching for answers
        that are right in front of us,
            if we would only look to you.
    Forgive us, holy One—
        for using hateful words
            instead of joyful acclamations;
        for taking violence for granted
            instead of promoting your peace and justice;
        for allowing darkness to overcome
            your radiant light.
    Loving God, help us turn our lives to you,
        that we may be ready when your Son is born,
            among us and within us. Amen.

Words of Assurance (Matthew 24:42 NRSV)
    Jesus proclaims, "Keep awake."
    Brothers and sisters, awaken to a new day—
        a day when our lives are filled with the forgiveness
        and the mercy of our loving God. Amen.

Passing the Peace of Christ (Psalm 122)
    Peace be within you!
    And also with you!

Let the peace within us be shared with one and all
as we share the peace of Christ with one another.

Introduction to the Word

Shine your light upon us, O God,
    that our lives may be illuminated
        by your holy story. Amen.

Response to the Word (Isaiah 2, Matthew 24)

Great God of peace,
    may we receive your words with open hearts,
        that our lives may be transformed by your love.
May we be prepared to follow you,
    and to live according to your ways.
And may our daily actions reflect your light
    for all humanity to see. Amen.

Advent Affirmation of Faith

We believe in the coming of the Light
    that shatters all darkness
    and brings love to all people.
We believe in peace, and that one day
    all nations shall enter the house of God,
        where love and mercy flow like a mighty river.
We believe in a hope that casts out fear.
We believe in waiting patiently
    for the coming of the Lord,
        knowing it is Christ who restores us
        and leads us to salvation.
We believe in being ready,
    for Christ comes at unexpected times and places,
    in the form of strangers, friends, and family.
We believe that we are called to welcome one another,
    just as Christ has welcomed us.

We believe that the Holy Spirit helps us
    live in harmony with one another,
    and prepare our hearts and our lives
    for the birth of a child who is called
    "Prince of Peace," "Emmanuel," "God with us."
Amen.

Thanksgiving and Communion

Invitation to the Offering (Matthew 24)
    Christ calls us to be ready when a guest arrives. Let us
    bring forth our gifts, so that this house, and our very
    lives, might be ready to receive the one who brings new
    life to all.

Offering Prayer (Isaiah 2)
    Holy One, take these gifts
        and turn them into merciful actions
            for your children everywhere.
    May these gifts be the spark
        that allows others to walk in your light,
            and to dwell in your love. Amen.

Sending Forth

Benediction
    Brothers and sisters, our Advent journey has begun!
    Go from this place worshipping the one
        who brings forth light and love, joy and hope.
    Go in peace. Amen.

December 4, 2016

Second Sunday of Advent

Mary J. Scifres

Color

Purple

Scripture Readings

Isaiah 11:1-10; Psalms 72:1-7, 18-19; Romans 15:4-13; Matthew 3:1-12

Theme Ideas

Growth is not an option for followers of God. Growth is our path—the straight path toward God, toward peace, toward love. Even from an old dead stump, God can raise up a shoot that will fulfill the promises given to our ancestors. Jesus is the new branch foretold by Isaiah, but so are the followers of Christ who take up the challenge to bear the fruit of God's Spirit. Signs of growth and life are all around us: in holiday decorations of evergreens and bright poinsettias; in Advent traditions of caring for the poor, giving to the needy, and sharing love freely and abundantly; in preparations to celebrate Christmas and the birth of the One who brings growth to all.

Invitation and Gathering

Contemporary Gathering Words (Matthew 3)
On the journey toward Christmas, God calls:
change your hearts, transform your lives,
and prepare the way of the Lord!

Call to Worship (Isaiah 11, Matthew 3)
As we prepare to grow with God,
we nurture love and understanding.
As we prepare to grow with Christ,
we bring forth justice and peace.
As we prepare to grow in the Spirit,
we live the promises of Christmas—
promises of love, peace, hope, and joy

Opening Prayer (Isaiah 11)
Nurture us with the bread of justice.
Strengthen us with wine of compassion and peace.
Shower us with wellspring of hope and promise,
Live in us this day,
that we may grow in stature and grace.
In Christ's name, we pray. Amen.

Proclamation and Response

Prayer of Confession (Matthew 3, Isaiah 11)
Holy Spirit, send your cleansing fire into our lives,
that we may bear the fruit of righteousness.
When we create division where peace is most needed,
lead us into the ways of life.
When we cling to old patterns that destroy,
straighten out the crooked roads
of doubt and despair.

When we harden our hearts against love and kindness,
    soften our hearts so that love guides our paths.
Grant us the peace that passes all understanding,
    and nourish us with hope and faith,
        that we might walk in your ways
          and bear the fruit of your love.

Words of Assurance (Isaiah 11)
    Christ is God's branch of mercy and grace—
        the promise of new life out of death and despair.
    In Christ, we are freed to begin anew,
        and to grow in the love of God!

Passing the Peace of Christ (Romans 15)
    Welcome one another in the same way that Christ has welcomed you. Welcome one another with grace, peace and love.

Introduction to the Word (Matthew 3)
    Prepare the way of Christ. Listen for the word of God.

Response to the Word (Isaiah 11)
    Wolves and lambs living together,
        leopards and goats taking a nap,
    calves and lions sharing a snack,
        babies and snakes playing in the desert—
    these are the crazy promises of God.
        These are the wildest dreams of God's people.
    Democrats and Republicans living together in joy,
        drug lords and mothers taking a peaceful nap,
    homeless families and mansion dwellers
    sharing an abundant feast,
        children and soldiers playing in the desert—
    these are the crazy promises of God.

These are the wildest dreams of Christmas.
May our Christmas dreams come true!

Thanksgiving and Communion

Invitation to the Offering (Psalm 72)
As we share our gifts with the people of God, we bring
forth justice for the poor, deliverance to the needy, and
hope to the oppressed.

Offering Prayer (Psalm 72, Advent)
Bless these gifts, O God,
  that they may become justice for the poor,
    deliverance to the needy,
      and hope to the oppressed.
Bless our gifts, Holy One,
  that we may grow in your grace,
    and produce the fruit of your Spirit:
      Love, peace, hope, and joy.

Sending Forth

Benediction (Romans 15)
May God fill you with peace.
May God fill you with joy.
May God bless you with hope and love.

December 11, 2016

Third Sunday of Advent
Joanne Carlson Brown

Color

Purple

Scripture Readings

Isaiah 35:1-10; Luke 1:47-55; James 5:7-10; Matthew 11:2-11

Theme Ideas

The world turned upside down...Miracles abounding...Communities and peoples restored. Patience urged...Must be Advent. The scriptures today speak of the world as God created it to be, as God wants it to be—God's dream for God's creation and peoples, God's dream to replace the nightmare that things have become. Advent is more than a time of expectation and waiting patiently. It is a time to embrace God's dream and God's vision of justice and love being the law of the land. It is a time for us to dedicate ourselves to be co-dreamers and co-workers with God, a time with Jesus to bring about God's beloved community, here and now. It is reassuring that not even fools can go astray if we walk God's Holy Way.

Invitation and Gathering

Contemporary Gathering Words (Isaiah 35, Luke 1)
The world is being turned upside down!
Where? I don't see it.
There's injustice and brokenness all around.
No, look! God is alive and active in the world.
I'm still having trouble believing that's true.
Give it a chance. Listen to God's promises
told in scripture and song. Join with the gang
as we head down God's Holy Way.

Call to Worship (Isaiah 35, Matthew 11)
Look and see the glory and majesty of our God.
Deserts rejoice and blossom
with joy and singing!
God will come and save God's people!
Healing will come to God's creation
and God's people!
—*Or*—

Call to Worship (Isaiah 35, Luke 1)
Come, let us magnify God in word and deed.
God is doing so many marvelous things.
Come, share in God's dream for us and for the world.
We come to hear and to learn
and to be prepared for the task ahead.
May this time of worship
lead us onto God's Holy Highway.
Come, let's dream, and then let's do.

Opening Prayer (Isaiah 35, Luke 1, Matthew 11)
God of transformation and love,
we come to this time of worship

yearning for a vision and the promise
of a better world.
Open our eyes, our ears, and our hearts,
to your dream of what you created us
and this world to be.
Strengthen us by what we see
in the actions of our sisters and brothers
with whom we worship.
Inspire us with a vision of walking your Holy Way—
a vision so compelling and so clear
that not even fools can go astray
if you walk with us on the journey
to create a world of justice,
radical love, and liberation.
May we sing with Mary, witness with Jesus,
and make your dream a reality. Amen.

Proclamation and Praise

Prayer of Confession (Isaiah 35, Luke 1, Matthew 11)
God of the Holy Way, we see the world as it is,
and despair in doing anything about it.
There will always be wars.
There will always be injustice.
There will always be pain and suffering.
Yes, Jesus worked miracles,
but that was him, and that was then.
Where is the hope now?
Help us catch your vision, your dream for the world—
as it should be, restored and whole,
blossoming abundantly.

Take us from despair to hope,
and from hope to action.
Let us live the song of Mary.
Let us preach the actions of Jesus.
Let us embody the prophecy of Isaiah.
Take from us our weak resignation
to the evils we deplore.
Help us realize that with you all things are possible,
and that with you guiding our way,
not even fools, like us, can go astray. Amen.

Words of Assurance (Isaiah 35)
God says to those who are fearful of heart:
Be strong, do not fear!
God is with us no matter what.
The time is coming when all will know joy and gladness,
when sorrow and sighing will flee away.

Passing the Peace of Christ (Isaiah 35)
Let us greet one another with this affirmation: Be strong
and do not fear, for God is here with us.

Prayer of Preparation (Isaiah 35, Luke 1, Matthew 11)
May we truly hear the good news preached,
not only to the poor, but to all God's peoples.
May the promises voiced in scripture
find root in our heart,
that it may blossom abundantly.

Response to the Word (Isaiah 35, Luke 1, James 5)
For the promises given,
for the strength imparted to our hearts,
for the vision of the Holy Way of God,
we give God thanks and praise.

Thanksgiving

Invitation to the Offering (Isaiah 35, Luke 1, Matthew 11)
We have been called to strengthen the weak, encourage
the faint of heart, and speak words of healing to a broken world. Our offering will enable this church to live
and walk God's Holy Way, inviting all to come and find
strength and healing and purpose and love.

Offering Prayer (Isaiah 35, Luke 1, Matthew 11)
Dreaming God, you have set before us
a vision of what can and should be
for your world and for your people.
Use these gifts of money and resources
to bring your vision to reality.
We offer ourselves and our work,
as embodiments of the promise,
the vision and the pledge
to bring your beloved community,
here and now. Amen.

Sending Forth

Benediction (Isaiah 35, Luke 1, Matthew 11)
The Holy Way of God lies before us—
a way even fools cannot stray from.
Let us walk God's Way,
with the strength and the promise of God
in our hearts,
with the song of Mary in our souls,
and with the example of Jesus to guide our steps.
Amen.

December 18, 2016

Fourth Sunday of Advent

B. J. Beu

Color

Purple

Scripture Readings

Isaiah 7:10-16; Psalm 80:1-7, 17-19; Romans 1:1-7;
Matthew 1:18-25

Theme Ideas

Isaiah promises the birth of Immanuel, God with us. The psalmist longs for restoration and the light of God's salvation. Joseph dreams of the child who will be called Emmanuel, God with us. And Paul witnesses to the blessings of this holy child. On the Sunday before Christmas, we speak of God with us—a child who brings light to our darkness, restoration to our ruin, and salvation to our lives.

Invitation and Gathering

Contemporary Gathering Words (Isaiah 7, Psalm 80, Matthew 1)
> Light has dawned and God's promised restoration is at hand. Glory to God in the highest. God is with us!

Call to Worship (Isaiah 7, Psalm 80, Matthew 1)
> Stir up your might, O God.
> **Come and save us.**
> Let your face shine upon us.
> **Give us a sign of the birth of Emmanuel,**
> One who will refuse the evil and choose the good.
> **A child of promise.**
> Stir up your might, O God.
> **Come and save us.**

Opening Prayer (Isaiah 7, Psalm 80)
> Lead us, Shepherd of Israel,
>> like you led your people of old.
> Long have we fed on the bread of tears,
>> and yearned to taste the joy of your presence.
> As we follow the child of promise,
>> the child of hope,
>> the child called Emmanuel, God with us,
>>> teach us to refuse the evil,
>>>> even as we strive to choose the good.

Proclamation and Response

Prayer of Confession (Isaiah 7, Psalm 80, Matthew 1)
> O God, we eagerly await the true light
>> that is coming into the world,

but we are easily distracted
by the twinkly lights all around us.
We planned to spend this season in study and prayer,
cultivating our interior life with you,
but we got distracted by the season's social demands.
Stir up your might, and shake us from our complacency,
that we might remember the reason for the season—
a child sent to bring us light and love,
a child sent to save us. Amen.

Assurance of Pardon (Isaiah 7, Romans 1, Matthew 1)
God is with us because God loves us.
God has always loved us.
Rest in this knowledge: God came to save us,
and God is with us.

Response to the Word (Matthew 1)
The One who visited Joseph in a dream visits us still.
The Spirit that was at work saving the Hebrew people
long ago is at work in our lives today. The child born of
Mary lives in our midst when we gather in his name.
God is with us, Emmanuel.

Thanksgiving and Communion

Offering Prayer (Psalm 80, Matthew 1)
Shepherd of Israel,
you have led us like a flock
into the pastures of your grace and mercy.
In thankfulness and praise
for the child born to us at Christmas,
receive the gift of our tithes and offerings.

Receive our hearts also,
    that we may share your love with the world. Amen.

Sending Forth

Benediction (Isaiah 7, Matthew 1)
    God has given us a sign—
        a child born for us and for our salvation.
    Go with anticipation and longing.
        We go with joy and hope,
        trusting in the promises of God.

December 24, 2016

Christmas Eve, Proper I

Mary J. Scifres

[Copyright © 2015 by Mary J. Scifres. Used by permission.]

Color

White

Scripture Readings

Isaiah 9:2-7; Psalm 96; Titus 2:11-14; Luke 2:1-20

Theme Ideas

After a busy season of preparing for the holiday, peace settles in on Christmas Eve—from our scriptures, from the candlelight, and from the quiet moment when we pause to worship. The Messiah will bring "endless peace," as promised by Isaiah in verse 7. The angels proclaim "peace on earth" as they celebrate the birth of Jesus, a promise echoed in the beloved carol "Silent Night": "All is calm. . . . Sleep in heavenly peace."

Invitation and Gathering

Centering Words (Titus 2, Isaiah 9, Luke 2)
We have been waiting for the blessed hope of Christmas, for the glorious appearance of Christ. Christ comes with promises of peace, hope, joy, and love.

Contemporary Gathering Words (Luke 2)
>Let's go right now to Bethlehem
>>and see what the shepherds saw.
>Let's go right now to see what's happened
>>and rejoice in the birth of Christ.
>Let's go right now to ponder with Mary,
>>to listen and remember,
>>and to rejoice in the miracle of Christmas.

Call to Worship (Psalm 96, Luke 2)
>Sing a new song of our ancient story.
>>**Sing of the birth of Christ.**
>Sing a new song of our ancient hope.
>>**Sing of the promises of God.**
>Sing a new song of peace and love.
>>**Sing with the angels above.**

Opening Prayer (Luke 2, Titus 2, Isaiah 9)
>God of endless peace,
>>bless us with the great light
>>>of your love and grace.
>Grant us your peace and hope,
>>as we sing of your glory
>>>and rejoice in the birth of your Son.
>In the precious name of Jesus, we pray. Amen.

Proclamation and Response

Prayer of Confession (Isaiah 9, Titus 2, Luke 2)
>When we are afraid,
>>comfort us with your presence.
>When we are weak,
>>support us with your strength.
>When we are lost and confused,
>>guide us with your wisdom and counsel.

THE ABINGDON WORSHIP ANNUAL 2016

When we are alone,
> draw us closer to you,
>> that we may recognize your presence.
Grant us your forgiveness and grace, O Prince of Peace,
> that in blessed hope,
>> we may know your endless peace. Amen.

Words of Assurance (Luke 2)
Don't be afraid! God has good news for us—
> wonderful, joyous news for all people!
The savior has been born for us—
> in our world, in our lives, in our hearts.
This is Christ the Lord,
> who brings forgiveness and peace.

Passing the Peace of Christ (Luke 2)
Glory to God and peace on earth.
Share this good news together.
Glory to God and peace on earth!

Introduction to the Word (Luke 2)
Don't be afraid! Look! Listen! God brings us good news, wonderful news for all people in the words of Christmas.

Response to the Word (Luke 2)
(Responses can be sung by a choir or soloist, or this litany may lead into the singing of a quiet lullaby such as "Still, Still, Still" or "Silent Night, Holy Night.")
Silent and still, we wait for God.
> **Still, still, still...**
Silent and still, we listen for God.
> **On this silent, holy night...**

Silent and still, we wait with hope.
Still, still, still...
Silent and still, we pray for peace.
On this silent, holy night...
Silent and still, we wait for God.
Still, still, still...

Thanksgiving and Communion

Invitation to the Offering (Luke 2)
Christ comes to newborn babies, angels and shepherds, sages and kings, old people and young. This ancient story comes with promises of peace and love for all. May our offering be a sign of peace and love as we share our gifts with God.

Offering Prayer (Luke 2)
Bring good news through these gifts, O God.
Through our love and generosity,
  spread wonderful, joyous news for all people,
    that all may sing of your glory
    and your peace on earth!

Sending Forth

Benediction (Luke 2)
Go in peace on this holy night.
We go with the peace of God.

December 25, 2016

Color

White

Scripture Readings

Isaiah 52:7-10; Psalm 98; Hebrews 1:1-4, (5-12); John 1:1-14

Theme Ideas

Although the birth of Jesus is the focus of Christmas, themes of grace and salvation abound in today's readings. These texts remind us to sing and rejoice, not only as we celebrate Christ's birth, but throughout the year. This need is as ancient as the word of God itself. Today, of all days, is a time to convey the glory of this ancient miracle and feel its enduring power to transform our lives.

Invitation and Gathering

Contemporary Gathering Words (Isaiah 52, Psalm 98)
Blessed are the feet of those who come announcing peace. Blessed are the mouths that share laughter and

joy. Blessed are the hearts that overflow with holy love. Blessed are the messengers who come proclaiming the miracle of Christ's birth.

Call to Worship (John 1, Psalm 98)
In the beginning was the Word,
and the Word was with God,
and the Word was God.
> **Make a joyful noise to the Lord, all the earth.**
> **Let the seas roar and the mountains quake.**
Everything came into being through the Word.
What came into being was life,
and the life was the light for all people.
> **Sing to the Lord a new song,**
> **for God has done marvelous things.**
The Word became flesh and blood,
and lived among us to bring all people to the light.
> **Let heaven and earth**
> **break forth into joyous song,**
> **singing praises to our God.**
The light shines in the darkness
and the darkness has not overcome it.
> **Christ, our light, shines forth in glory.**
> **Christ, our life, brings grace and truth.**
> **Let us worship. Alleluia!**

Opening Prayer (Isaiah 52, Psalm 98, John 1)
How beautiful upon the mountains, O God,
are messengers of your light and love
who come announcing peace.
How delightful in the congregation
are voices singing the good news
of our salvation.

How wonderful in the wretched places of our world
    are heralds of your justice and mercy
        who proclaim the coming of your reign.
Bring us your peace, Holy One,
    and remind us once more
        of the good news of our salvation,
            that we might sing with joy this day,
                and shout for all the world to hear.
Christ is born. Alleluia!

Proclamation and Response

Prayer of Confession (Isaiah 52, Hebrews 1)
    God of new beginnings,
        when our eyes become fixed
            on the glitz of the season,
                turn our gaze once more to the hills,
                    where your messengers come
                        bringing news of hope and peace;
        when our attention becomes trapped
            in bitter conflicts of the past,
                remind us once more,
                    that you speak a freeing word to us
                    through your Son.
    Free us from the surface trappings of this day,
        and refocus our hearts
            on the glory of Christ's birth,
                that we may be messengers of peace
                and children of your Spirit. Amen.

Words of Assurance (Psalm 98, Hebrews 1)
    With righteousness and equity,
        Christ has come to bring justice and grace,
        love and compassion.

Through the tender mercies of our God,
    and the glorious love of Jesus Christ,
    we are forgiven!

Passing the Peace of Christ (Isaiah 52)

How beautiful are the feet of those who come announcing peace. How radiant are the eyes of those who shine the light of God's love. With blessings of peace and love to share, let us turn to one another and offer signs of God's blessings this Christmas day.

Thanksgiving and Communion

Invitation to the Offering (Isaiah 52)

In a cynical world that puts personal well-being ahead of the common good, let us remind the skeptics of the beauty of messengers who come proclaiming peace. Let us show the doubters that we, the people of God, truly do believe what we profess. Let us share the gifts we have received from God, that others might know that Christ is alive in our hearts, and is born anew in us each day as we share Christ's love with one another.

Offering Prayer (Hebrews 1, John 1)

God of light and love,
    receive our gifts this day,
        and strengthen our commitment
            to share the love we feel at Christmas
                with those in need throughout the year.
Send these offerings into the world
    on the wings of your angels,
        that those who are touched by our gifts

may feel the healing warmth
of your holy fire.
Shine in our lives and in our ministries,
that the whole world may see
your joyous light. Amen.

Sending Forth

Benediction (Isaiah 52, Psalm 98, John 1)
Make a joyful noise to the Lord.
We will sing praises to our God.
Walk in the light of Christ.
We will share the joy of God's holy love.
Be messengers of hope and peace.
We will proclaim the good news.
Christ is born. Alleluia!

Contributors

Laura Jaquith Bartlett, an ordained minister of music and worship, lives at a United Methodist adult retreat center in the foothills of Oregon's Mount Hood, where she serves as the program director, as well as doing worship consulting and coaching.

B. J. Beu is senior pastor of Neighborhood Congregational Church in Laguna Beach, California. A graduate of Boston University and Pacific Lutheran University, Beu loves creative worship, preaching, and advocating for peace and justice. Find out more at B. J.'s church website www .ncclaguna.org

Susan A. Blain is Minister for Worship, Liturgy, and Spiritual Formation with Local Church Ministries of the United Church of Christ. Sue works with writers and liturgists from around the UCC to create *Worship Ways*, the on-line resource for lectionary-based worship. She has edited volumes 2 and 3 of *Imaging the Word: An Arts and Lectionary Resource* © 1995 and 1996 United Church Press. She served on the editorial board for *Sing! Prayer and Praise* © 2009 Pilgrim Press.

Mary Petrina Boyd is pastor of Langley United Methodist Church on Whidbey Island. She spends alternating summers working as an archaeologist in Jordan.

Joanne Carlson Brown is the clergy-type for Tibbetts United Methodist Church in Seattle, Washington. She is also an adjunct professor at Seattle University School of Theology and Ministry and lives in Seattle with Thistle, the wee Westie.

Karen Ellis is a United Methodist pastor who lives in Tustin, California with her husband and two children.

Safiyah Fosua serves as assistant professor of Christian Ministry and Congregational Worship at Wesley Seminary at Indiana Wesleyan University and is a clergy member of the Greater New Jersey Annual Conference.

Rebecca E. Garrett serves as a worship enlivener and director of music and worship arts in the North Texas area.

Rebecca J. Kruger Gaudino, a United Church of Christ minister in Portland, Oregon, teaches world religions and biblical studies as visiting professor at the University of Portland and also writes for the Church.

Jamie Greening is a Southern Baptist pastor and writer who blogs at www.jdgreening.wordpress.com.

Bill Hoppe is the music coordinator for Bear Creek United Methodist Church in Woodinville, Washington, and is a member of the band BrokenWorks, for which he is the keyboardist. He thanks his family and friends for their continued love, support, and inspiration.

Amy B. Hunter is a poet, spiritual director, and Episcopal layperson. Her work tends to be Christian formation, but her passion is answering God's call to her to write. Two out-comes of her writing life are *A Table in the Wilderness*, avail-able at Lulu.com, and a blog, Astrolabe and Trope (http://astrolabeandtrope.wordpress.com/).

Mary J. Scifres serves as a consultant in church lead-ership, worship, and evangelism from her Laguna Beach home, where she and her spouse B. J. reside with their teenage son, Michael. Her books include *The United Meth-odist Music and Worship Planner, Just in Time Special Services, Prepare!* and *Searching for Seekers*. Find out more at Mary's website, www.maryscifres.com

Deborah Sokolove is associate professor of Art and Wor-ship at Wesley Theological Seminary where she also serves as the director of the Henry Luce III Center for the Arts and Religion.

Leigh Anne Taylor is the minister of music at Blacksburg United Methodist Church and lives with her family in the mountains of southwest Virginia. She has recently pub-lished a book that she co-wrote with her former husband Rev. Joe Cobb, *Our Family Outing, A Memoir of Coming Out and Coming Through*.

John van de Laar is a Methodist minister, the founding director of Sacredise.com, and the author of *The Hour That Changes Everything* and *Learning to Belong*.

Indexes

Page numbers in italics refer to the online-only material.

Scripture Index

Communion Liturgies

Liturgies in italics are online-only material.

For download access to the online material, click on the link for *The Abingdon Worship Annual 2016* at abingdonpress.com/downloads, and when prompted, enter the password: worship2016.